You Can Be Funny and Make People Laugh

Also available

The Small Talk Code: The Secrets of Highly Successful Conversationalists

How to Talk Business Like a Boss: 53 Proven Techniques for Conquering Any Work Situation

My old sketchbook from 3rd grade art class. Just kidding, I have no idea where I put that thing.

You Can Be Funny and Make People Laugh

No Theories. No Fluff. 35 Humor Techniques that Work for Everyday Conversations.

Geoffrey "Gregory" Peart, M.Ed.

Aurelius Books

AURELIUS

Aurelius Books

Brighton, MI 48116

contact@aureliusbooks.com

greg@socialupgrader.com

This publication is designed to provide accurate and authoritative information in regard to the subject matter covered. It is sold with the understanding that the author is not a licensed therapist, and all advice is based on his own experiences. If you need professional help, please seek out resources in your area.

The names in my examples have been changed for privacy reasons.

How to be funny and make people laugh: No theories. No fluff. 35 humor techniques that work for everyday conversations/ Geoffrey "Gregory" Peart —1st ed.

ISBN-13: 978-1-7321791-6-5

To all the friends and family who made me laugh when times were tough. And to all the friends and family who made me laugh when times were easy. You all taught me how to appreciate the joy in the world. For that, I am eternally grateful.

To Mr. Elmleaf, my 7th grade math teacher: You tried so hard to get this overly serious guy to laugh, but I never cracked a smile. One time, you pulled me to the side after class and gave me a special homework assignment: "Go home, find something you think is funny, and come back and tell me what it is." I was too shy and serious to listen to your advice at that time, but I've always remembered what you told me, Mr. Elmleaf. I may be a little late completing my homework, but I hope this book counts.

The Contents

Section 4 - Entertain

Section 5 - Tell Stories

Hey, Want to Hear a Joke?

Americans type the keywords "knock knock jokes" into Google searches more than 368,000 times a month. In case you were wondering, I checked out how often Americans type *"killer* knock knock jokes," and it's 590 times a month (as of May 2019). If I wanted to kill my conversations, killer knock-knock jokes would certainly be my verbal weapon of choice.

The unfortunate (and unfunny) reality is that reciting jokes from joke books won't make you funny. Every time my father-in-law starts a conversation with, "Hey, did you hear the joke about..." part of me dies inside. I know the joke he's about to tell won't be funny because contrived jokes rarely ever are. However, because he's my father-in-law and because I'm a polite, well-mannered person, I force a smile and a pity laugh so he can save face and we can continue arguing about politics.

This book is about conversational humor, or how to add a little appropriate fun and playfulness into a conversation so that the people involved end up relating to each other better and feeling better connected. Conversational humor is more than just setups and punchlines—it's complicated. Save the scripted jokes for comedians. Instead, focus your mental energy on practicing and remembering techniques that can be naturally applied to everyday social situations. I just might know 35 of those kinds of techniques perfectly suited for conversations.

I'll be honest: you won't like all the techniques in this book. In fact, you'll probably think some of the examples are silly, strange, or downright stupid. But the good news is you'll also love some of them and think some of the examples are hilarious. And that's the thing about humor; it's not a one-size-fits-all type of deal.

I find the subtle glances that the characters exchange on the popular show, *The Office,* hilarious—but my wife looks at me like I'm crazy when I laugh at them. There's a reason no one in history has nailed down a universally-accepted definition of humor; it's a futile exercise because what people find funny differs from person to person and from situation to situation. You'd have better luck trying to herd a clowder of cats (Did you know that a group of cats is called a *clowder?* Seriously. I didn't believe it either.)

Unfortunately, some humor will naturally get lost in translation and in print form, and that's a risk I'm taking with this book. The delivery of the line, the energy, the mood, the inflections, and the personalities of the other people listening (and how many Gin and Tonics they drank that night) all factor into whether the comment is funny or dog-doo.

You'll just have to take my word that every example included in this book had the effect of making someone laugh at some point. If or when you come across an example that you don't find particularly funny, try to revise or restate it in a way that is funny to you. It will help you develop your own humorous style or voice.

2

Full disclosure: Unless you count that one time my little brother paid me a quarter to hear a joke, I'm not a professional comedian. I'm just someone who really wanted to learn how to be funny, and I became fascinated (my wife would say *completely obsessed*) with studying funny people. After spending fifteen years writing down and analyzing more than 17,000 conversations, a number of techniques emerged from the small talk rubble that I found useful, and I think you will, too.

I didn't personally create the techniques. It's more like I discovered them; I was just fortunate enough to be exposed to a lot of funny people over the years. After years of note-taking, studying, and analyzing, I was able to identify certain common characteristics that seemed to get a smile or a laugh. As a result of practicing the techniques in my own conversations, my ability to make people laugh increased until it eventually became second nature. But it wasn't always easy.

Travel back in time with me for a minute. When I was sixteen, a girl sitting at my table in art class turned toward me and remarked ever so politely, "You should try to find a personality." She was trying to offer advice, but her words hit me like a ton of bricks. I knew I was shy, but I didn't think my shyness was to the point that random people felt pity for me, like I was some down-and-out stray dog needing a hug and some leftover chicken wings. Where does one "find" a personality anyway? Last I checked, Amazon wasn't selling those yet. Her insensitive adolescent comment jumpstarted my journey into the self-improvement world.

Fast-forward to age thirty-one, and I'm in a meeting with a colleague. She remarks, "You know what I like about you? I appreciate that you can be really funny without being negative toward other people. That kind of humor is really rare." That was the greatest compliment I had received in years. I thought to myself, "*Mission accomplished!*" Not only was I rapidly ascending in my career and socially confident, but it was official: I was officially deemed "funny."

I've written other social skills books, but I consider humor to be the most advanced and most life-changing topic. There's a reason it's so highly coveted: humor is power. Humor helps build connections and relationships in ways that few other social interactions can. It makes all participants feel good (laughing naturally releases dopamine). It brings people together in shared positive experiences that are memorable and lasting. You may be one of the millions of people who have *paid* for the chance to listen to someone make them laugh. A good sense of humor has been the secret behind millions of relationships, marriages, business deals, happiness, and all kinds of other good stuff in life.

One thing I've noticed is that the majority of humor books are for aspiring comedians or comedy writers. There's a serious lack of books for people who just want to use humor to improve their everyday conversations. I set out to write just that, completely disregarding the famous quote by E.B. White:

> Analyzing humor is like dissecting a frog. Few people are interested, and the frog dies of it.

My mission here was to prove Mr. White wrong. By removing all the theoretical fluff, I think humor techniques are indeed relevant and interesting to read about. And don't worry, no frogs were killed in the making of this book.

I decided to take the opposite approach of other books; my book focuses on techniques and examples that can be applied to everyday conversations. You don't need to practice every technique, but it's important to spend the time on those you find most useful to your life and sense of humor. (Maybe even venture outside of your comfort zone a bit.) Like playing a sport, once you learn the technique, it will become second nature to you, and your brain can focus on other important things. Practice first in situations that are more socially comfortable for you, such as with close friends and family, or even with complete strangers you'll never see again. Take advantage of opportunities to small talk with anyone in customer service, because they're paid to talk to you!

If you're truly aware of your audience, the situation, and the mood, you can aim your humor far more effectively and increase your chance of success. The same humorous statement can fall flat with one person and strike gold with another, so don't always give up if your funny comment didn't get anywhere the first time.

Try to avoid giving up and waving the white flag too early; don't lose energy, trail off, and/or cut yourself off before seeing things all the way through. Remember, if you *act* like it's funny, then it's *more likely to be* funny and get the reaction you're looking for. If you act like it's not funny, and if you deliver it like you're nervous or overly serious, your audience will pick up on that feeling of trepidation. Someone gave me this tip decades ago and I wish I listened earlier: *Smile more.* Being funny is a choice. And if you're attempting humor, it's important to commit to it.

As a general suggestion, try to stay away from too much negative or cruel humor. If your friends are a bunch of sarcastic critics or internet trolls, sure, throw them a few bones and they'll feast. However, humor tainted with arrogance or malice may offend instead of charm. There's enough sadness in the world. What we all need is more laughter.

5

Section 1

Lighten Up

Technique #1
Be Anyone But Literal Larry
Literal, serious, and predictable comments are never funny. Tap into your inner child and learn to play more.

Real-life Example

One day at work, I was preparing a room for a presentation, when my colleague Larry came in to help. I thought the room felt too hot, so I asked him, "Does the room feel a little too hot to you?" He responded, "Definitely, it seems very hot."

Pretty normal interaction, right? Another person, Patty, came in right after and I asked the same question. With a playfully dramatic tone of voice, she enthusiastically responded, "*Oh yeah! I feel like I just walked into the Amazon rainforest.*" We all laughed. And she didn't stop there. As she smiled and used her body language to exaggerate her playfulness, she continued moments later, "I think I've sweated off five pounds already!" We laughed again.

Why It Works

Playful Patty clearly knew how to employ exaggeration as a humor technique; she exaggerated both her words and her nonverbal delivery. She exaggerated how hot the room felt and how it affected her. She made a conscious decision to avoid responding literally and seriously and took some liberties to play around.

Larry gave a polite comment, certainly, but it didn't inspire further playful conversation. His response was simple, direct, safe—and unengaging. If your goal is to be funny, don't be bland and predictable.

Literal Larrys often wonder why they can't be funny. The thing is, funny people are always looking for alternative, playful ways to comment and engage in conversations. Playful people aren't always in a playful mood, of course (they, too, can wake up on the wrong side of the bed), and they don't always strike gold, but being playful at least puts them in a position to elicit laughter. Patty figured we might laugh if she exaggerated her response, and she was right.

Direct questions, like, "Where are you going?" or "What are you doing?" are perfect opportunities for experimenting with unanticipated humorous responses. The question-asker is likely expecting a literal answer, so a lighthearted and funny response could result in easy humor simply because it's unexpected.

My boss recently needed to order everyone shirts with the company logo and asked me, "What size shirt are you?" I could have stuck with the literal, "I'm a large," but there's nothing funny about that. Instead, with a look of self-deprecating guilt, I answered, "It depends how much I ate for breakfast," which kept the mood in more playful territory. Of course, I eventually told him my actual shirt size, but that's not the point.

Rather than describe a situation in literal terms, such as, "The printer isn't working well today," with the right tone, timing, and body language, funny people may apply a fun exaggerated twist, like, "The printer must not have gotten enough sleep last night because it's so cranky today!" Or, "I'm currently fighting a battle with the printer... and the printer is winning. I might need reinforcements."

Again, you're not going to make someone laugh every time with every humor technique. The point is to position the social interaction near or within the play zone so you at least have a chance at creating humor. And that starts with not being literal all the time.

The reality is, over the years, as you've matured, you've constructed filters that block the authentic, playfulness of your inner child. Your brain has constructed internal warning signs and flashing lights alerting you to every possible risk of every possible word and action. "Don't say that—she may not like it," or, "If you say that, you'll look dumb." So, what eventually comes out of your mouth is safe and predictable. The bad news is: humor and fun don't live in the safe and predictable. You have to be okay with a handful of randomness and a pinch of silliness. Remember what the great Robin Williams once said, "You're only given a little spark of madness; you mustn't lose it."

There's a risk involved with humor. If you're not ready to take chances, I encourage you to take baby steps along this book's journey. Find your voice by trying the techniques and becoming more comfortable with them. The alternative is just plain depressing: Literal Larry stays home, goes to bed and then complains, "Nothing fun or interesting ever happens to me." Whereas Playful Peggy sometimes stays out late, visits new places, talks to new people, and creates adventures. She may not always have fun or always have a good time, but she puts herself in position to have fun. She takes chances on things that aren't predictable. And meanwhile, Literal Larrys never seem to have entertaining stories to tell. Remember, you can't expect to memorize a bunch of techniques and hope to suddenly be funny. If you lack rich life experiences, and if you don't read much and lack thoughtful opinions, then trying to apply humor techniques to your conversations is the equivalent of trying to build a house in the wetlands of Louisiana.

Technique #2

Laugh at Yourself First

If you're too insecure and uptight, you'll have a hard time making anyone laugh (even Jimmy Fallon—and he laughs at everything).

Real-life Example

> Jack: Wow, that's an awesome tattoo.
>
> Jill: Thanks, my husband George actually drew it.
>
> Jack: Really? That's cool.

Not a very funny interaction, huh? What if Jack playfully admitted a weakness instead?

> Jack: Really? I wish I could draw like that—I could probably draw a stick figure, but that's about it. My skills don't get much beyond sticks—and half the time I can't even draw straight lines!

Why It Works

If you want to be funny, you need to be able to laugh at yourself first. Think about your favorite comedian—there's a strong chance he or she relies on a heavy dose of self-deprecating humor—they know their own weaknesses or shortcomings and aren't afraid to point them out in a humorous way. It's easily one of the most common comedic techniques.

Now think about the person or people who make you feel comfortable. Likable and easy-going people are usually comfortable in their own skin and have embraced their character flaws. They are okay with being a little vulnerable. Such people are the first to admit they aren't perfect and are happy to laugh at their personal quirks. They're quick to admit funny mistakes or episodes of forgetfulness. They use their flaws to their advantage.

One of the most likable and funny actors in Hollywood is Jennifer Lawrence because she's not afraid to laugh at herself and her mistakes. Check out the *Recommended Viewing* section at the end of the book for some great unscripted clips of her just being her genuine and quirky self to understand fully her allure.

Beautiful actors with arrogant personalities don't attract many fans. Few people want to listen to a braggart rave about how well he did on a test or how many sports cars he owns. But everyone enjoys hearing about the time you made a fool of yourself at that party—especially if you can laugh about it after the fact. Being okay with (and poking fun at) your own flaws helps you let your guard down, and it lets others take their guards down, too. It's a small reminder that nobody's perfect and that we're all in this together—*and that's ok*—that's the message you're sending. The end result is that people will often like you *more* after you expose an inner flaw or embarrassing experience, even of the small or trivial variety. Funny people realize their weaknesses and insecurities can actually make some interesting and entertaining conversation material.

In the olden days—I mean, in the days before GPS—I was riding in a car with my new boss, and she asked me how to find our destination. I responded rather bluntly, "I'll be honest, I'm navigationally impaired... I'm probably the worst person to ask for directions. If I say turn 'left,' you're probably better off turning 'right!'" She quickly admitted that she, too, was horrible at navigating, and we both had a few laughs over who was worse! It was a great bonding experience.

Don't take yourself too seriously if you want to be funny. My parents are great examples of this. Every time we go out to a restaurant, without fail, my father tries to crack a joke with the server. We never know what it will be, but like the inevitably of taxes and death, my father will try to be funny with restaurant staff. It falls flat half the time (he's British, so his humor doesn't always translate to American audiences—at least that's what he tells himself). My mother, without fail, acts embarrassed by her husband. And what do I do? I sit back and enjoy the show.

The restaurant example with my parents is a great microcosm of this technique in a nutshell. Pop quiz: how many times do you think my mother made the server at a restaurant laugh? That's right—zero times. Now, even though he embarrassed himself on occasion, my father made servers laugh sometimes. Which, for him, made any embarrassment worth it. He's able to brush off any awkwardness with ease because he's the first to laugh at himself if a joke backfires. My father taught me the value of being able to laugh at yourself; it's a foundational requirement if you want to make others laugh.

Meanwhile, my mother tends to over-worry about what others think of her. I was like that once, too, and I know many of you reading this book assume people are always judging your every move. And until you learn to laugh at yourself a little and learn to accept your shortcomings and quirks, you'll have a tough time trying to make others laugh. (To be fair, my mother is a classic introvert, and like a lot of introverts, opens up and is very funny when surrounded by people she knows well.)

I was chatting recently with comedian Sarah Cooper, and her number one tip for being funny in conversation was to start with *honesty*. Be transparent first, and the funny will come. I thought that was great advice. A perfectly groomed man sitting next to you wearing a perfectly fitted suit isn't funny. But if the perfectly groomed man in a perfectly fitted suit accidentally squirts Dijon mustard on his pant leg, now there's potential for funny. Don't be afraid to take off your mask and show people your flaws. A magic thing happens when you take down your façade; you help others loosen up as well. The social tensions melt away, and the playfulness and fun seep into the interaction.

What are some of the imperfect traits, feelings, and behaviors behind your hard exterior? Irrational fears can be hilarious—what's one of yours? Afraid of cockroaches? Talk about how you'll never travel to NYC because you heard about how many cockroaches live there. Even though you may have a serious fear, you realize that it might be a little irrational, but you're inviting others to laugh at you regardless.

What about recovering from a verbal blunder? Be quick to admit your mistake and make light of it next time. Arming yourself with a few comments that help you recover from mistakes will help you bounce back from mistakes (don't think about that too hard, folks). The next time you find yourself flustered or embarrassed by a mistake, try turning the anxious situation into a lighthearted event with a self-deprecating comment like:

> That story seemed so much better in my head.
>
> That's the first thing that popped into my head... I need to work on my internal filters!
>
> Evidently, it was *not* a smart move for me to skip coffee this morning!
>
> We shouldn't take my car—it will probably break down on the way there!

I just completely butchered that expression, didn't I?

I probably should have proofread more that before sending it. Now you think I can't spell above a 4th grade level!

When you take advantage of mistakes instead of ignoring them, you're more likely to venture down fun and engaging tangents rather than experiencing awkward moments. Attempting humor is not easy because it's not predictable—the risk involved can be unsettling and scary. That's why it's so important to be able to laugh at your mistakes—because mistakes are inevitable. (Sometimes, the mistake is the funniest part!) If you're constantly afraid of making a mistake, you'll never be funny. But if you learn to laugh at yourself, or your failed attempt at being funny, or your botched storytelling, or your awkward impersonations, you'll begin to have the ability to make people laugh.

Technique #3

Don't Be an Energy Vampire

The difference between funny and "meh," and between engaging and unengaging, often comes down to the nonverbal delivery of the words and not the words themselves.

Real-life Example

This technique is about nonverbal delivery, so the only example that works here is one you can watch and listen to. First, read what comedian Aziz Ansari says in one of his skits:

> Has anyone tried to make plans with anyone? It's the most frustrating experience. 'Cause what happens anytime you ask someone to do something nowadays? It's like, 'Hey, you wanna do this fun thing?' 'Maybe... maybe, I could try.'

Why It Works

On the surface, there isn't any funny to be found, right? However, the audience nonetheless laughed the hardest at the word "maybe." Surprised? Sure, the writing may have resonated with the crowd, but the magic was in the nonverbal delivery of the words. *How* Aziz spoke transported his crowds to another time and place, where they could fully imagine themselves being in the situation he described. His character impersonations are incredibly believable and engaging.

Aziz is also a master of taking his listeners on auditory roller-coaster rides; full of highs and lows, slow build-ups and fast releases. He alternates between softly caressing some words and blasting energy at others. My description will never do him justice, so just for you, I've included all the referenced links to YouTube videos in the Recommended Viewing at the end of the book.

The success of a joke or story always comes down to how the words are delivered and not just the words themselves. Some of the lamest jokes and dullest stories can sparkle if told by great communicators. I once worked with an associate named Jane who frequently told stories about her young children. Jane always included mundane details in her stories about toddlers refusing to take baths or dropping peanut butter on the floor. However, the way she became absorbed in the story and told it with such playful enthusiasm is what always made her stories so engaging and entertaining.

The opposite is true, too—you may have brilliant comments or delightful stories in your head, but if you express yourself in an uninteresting way, don't be surprised if others find you boring and uninteresting.

The more playful energy and enthusiasm you put into a social interaction, the more of it you'll see reflected back from the other person. We often laugh with friends not because of the content of what they said, but because they said it like it was supposed to be funny. Often, we start smiling before the other person finishes, because they are telling us something with such great enthusiasm and levity that we expect to laugh, and we sometimes do just because it feels like we should. However, if you were to write down what was said and read it again later, the words themselves often wouldn't be very funny on their own.

Think about a person in your life who isn't fun to be around. Why aren't they any fun? I'm guessing it's because they're either mean, selfish, or boring. This book can't help you with the *mean* or *selfish* part, but *boring* can be fixed. Boring people either don't have anything interesting to say, or they speak without any enthusiasm, or both. Think Toby Flenderson from *The Office* (NBC, 2005-2013). He had such little energy, and offered nothing of substance to conversations, that he was generally an insufferable bore who drove Michael Scott crazy throughout the entire series. The Office fans out there may argue that Angela Martin was just as boring, and in addition, was generally mean-spirited and never contributed positively to any interaction. I wouldn't disagree with that assessment. She would even go so far as to intentionally deflate the merry mood. Don't be like Toby or Angela. Kevin Malone was low-energy too, but at least he generally maintained a good attitude.

Ask yourself, do you more often add energy to a social interaction, or suck it away like an energy vampire? If you're sucking the energy out of situations, or if you're hard to hear or understand, nothing you say will make a difference. You might as well go back to your crypt. Ultimately, if you're more Toby than Michael, I suggest you work extra hard on this technique because the consequences will be life-changing.

Your visual body language also matters. Are you stiff as a board when speaking or are you animated? As humans, we like visual stimulation, so when you're speaking, make sure you move a bit, employ some gestures, and leverage the different expressions your face is capable of.

I can't stress this enough: If you simply improve your delivery, you don't need to learn a single new comedic technique or joke because everything you say will be naturally more entertaining and you'll notice a difference immediately. Start noticing if you trail off at the end of your comments. Do you make an effort to emphasize the key parts of your story with extra enthusiasm? If not, you should start.

Homework

Homework?? Sorry, I forgot to mention earlier that I occasionally add in homework to certain techniques because I'm a teacher at heart, and I believe in the value of practice.

I strongly suggest improving your energy and your nonverbal delivery before attempting any other technique. Let's be honest, there's no point in learning anything else if you can't deliver the words effectively. Get on YouTube (see Recommend Viewing at the end of the book) and practice imitating masters like Aziz until you develop your own style.

Next, record yourself telling a story; listen and watch *how* you deliver the words. Do this over and over until you notice improvement and find a style of delivery that works for your personality. Professional comedians do the same thing: they try the same material over and over with slight variations to refine their jokes until they're maximally funny.

Section 2

Observe

Technique #4

The Humor's in the Details (Just Not Too Many, Okay?)

If you want to be funny, you'll need to upgrade the way you describe things—like your surroundings, yourself, and your annoying little brother.

Real-life Examples

Examine the following comparisons. The first comments express the thought using the bare minimum description. The second comments elaborate the thought more colorfully.

1. "His breath smelled so bad!" vs. "His breath smelled like beef stroganoff!"
2. "There were a lot of people there." vs. "It was like Woodstock all over again, but with less mud and naked people."

Why It Works

Saying "His breath smelled *bad*" isn't nearly as funny as saying "His breath smelled like *beef stroganoff*." Some words are inherently more interesting than others (possibly because they're less commonly used or unexpected). Regardless of the meaning, the phrase "beef stroganoff" just sounds funny by itself. You could substitute "beef stroganoff" with "gorgonzola cheese" or "moldy elderberries" and it would probably still work. Pay attention to what your circle of friends thinks is funny and sprinkle those words into your vernacular.

Have you ever wondered why someone else can say the same basic thing you did but receive a much better reaction? The disparity may occur because of subtle differences in delivery, such as timing, emphasis and intonation (also known as prosody), energy, personal style, etc. But sometimes, it comes down to just one or two key words. A single keyword can often make or break a phrase, joke, or story. You may think that is obvious, but subpar conversationalists often underestimate the power of words and choose boring and easy instead of fun and interesting.

Advertisers and good writers know that incorporating visual imagery, analogies, and emotive words are among the fastest ways to your heart (and wallet!). That's also why most sports broadcasts have "color commentators." Fans don't just want the facts. They want the emotions that go along with the game. They connect with the colorful descriptions!

If I described an old man as "grumpy," it would be sufficient. You'd get it. But what if I painted a picture that was even more descriptive and relatable? "He had this grumpy, sour face." That's better. Here's another option: "He had this grumpy, just-drank-apple-cider-vinegar look." Can you visualize him a little better now?

Even something as mundane and unpleasant as changing a dirty diaper contains moments of levity and fun if you play with your descriptions. There is an entire range of experiences, from the easy-clean-up to the total nuclear disaster; the more extreme the mess, the more options are available for colorful descriptions. You could say little Rowan let loose a *torrential flood of toxic waste. 100% liquid. Flammable liquid. Napalm.* Talk about how you might need a *hazmat suit* just to survive, and that you may suffocate soon from the *poisonous fumes.* Have fun. Play. Color.

The following two statements are in response to a friend complaining about a jerk boyfriend. They say basically the same thing, except for one difference.

> Does he think you're going to make his *breakfast* every morning too?

> Does he think you're going to make his *peanut butter protein shake* every morning too?

In conversation, the second version will always be more interesting and funnier than the first version. Why? It's more descriptive. And obviously, it's not poetic verse either—adding *even one detail* is often sufficient.

Colorful words trigger emotions and mental images. Boring words do not. There's power in that. However, everything you say doesn't need to be colorful or bursting with flavor. The goal is to strike a balance between a few boring words and too many detailed words. Were you ever forced to read *War and Peace* (Leo Tolstoy, 1869) in school? Fun fact: Tolstoy himself didn't like the novel. He confessed to being happy that he "won't have to write such wordy nonsense ever again." War and Peace is so full of rambling sentences that you forget the beginning by the time you come to the end. If you speak like the way Leo Tolstoy wrote, you're probably overdoing it on the details.

Let's unpack that protein shake example a little more. There was another key part that made it entertaining: the words "every morning." Look at it again *without* such exaggerated language: "Does he think you're going to make his breakfast sometimes, too?" "Occasionally," "sometimes" and other qualifiers don't pack the same punch as strong definitive words, like "every" and "always." On top of that, if you emphasized the keywords with extra enthusiasm and energy, you'd see even better results.

One time a colleague handed me a plain-looking birthday card. As she handed it to me, she stated, "Sorry, the store ran out of the cool cards. No one should ever get a burgundy-colored birthday card." I couldn't help but chuckle. Now my colleague could have said instead, "Sorry, the store ran out of interesting cards. This card isn't great for birthday cards and is oddly colored." Both remarks say essentially the same thing, but the former version is 10X more entertaining. One reason is because my colleague included the more visual (and inherently fun-sounding) keyword "burgundy." The other reason is because the former version contained more absolute language: "No one should ever..." Exaggerated language will always be more entertaining than overly accurate and neutral language.

Literal, objective description is safer, but unfortunately it's boring. Think about when someone asks a question like, "What do you do?" You may feel inclined to answer literally and directly. "I'm a chemistry teacher." Instead of saying "I'm a chemistry teacher," try more *figurative*, colorful descriptions, like, "I basically teach kids how to play with poisons."

When you add more colorful words, you'll inspire others to play along too. For example, Henry and Margie are out for a walk. Henry doesn't have to say the word "swanky" to describe the bar across the street, but when he does, Margie capitalizes on it.

Henry: I think that's the *swanky* bar all the rich people go to.

Margie: Yeah, you're right. I can smell the *swank* from here —kind of sour, like rotten milk.

Notice how they end up creating a funny interaction *together*. And what's better than that? Humor doesn't need to be a solo sport—become better at helping others create humor too by experimenting with more interesting ways to describe people, actions, surroundings, and things—you never know what word someone else will grab on to.

Look at the following exchange:

> Justin: Before you come over, I've gotta clean up the place.
>
> Melissa: Don't worry, that's fine. I don't care if there's a mess anywhere.

Pretty standard conversation, right? It would have been funny if Melissa added some details:

> Melissa: Don't worry, that's fine. I'm no Martha Stewart—I couldn't care less if you left out a plate of two-week-old macaroni or something.

Now Justin is more likely to play along and has more options to connect to in order to continue the conversation. Justin could respond to the *Martha Stewart* keyword or the *macaroni* keyword, for example, "Good, because I think *Martha Stewart would faint* the minute she walked through my door!"

Word Mix-ups

Say you're a parent at an event with other parents and kids. The kids are making crafts in a room and the parents are at the side, sitting in chairs watching. (If you don't have kids yet, just wait, this will be your future.) You could walk to the section with the parents and make conversation by stating, "This must be where the parents sit." But that's pretty boring. A more interesting version would be,

"This must be *the parent's lounge*." The words "parent" and "lounge" are not found together in the wild, but creating a new term like that is fun and interesting. In addition, it conjures up an image of a glamorous resting place that is the complete opposite of a row of cold metal folding chairs against a wall.

Some of my friends had a funny conversation about the History channel recently.

> Dave: What's up with the History channel not showing much history—*it's just Nazis and Aliens now.*
>
> Andy: What do you mean? That is our history. Whether you like it or not. Aliens and Nazis.
>
> Kenny: And don't forget about *Alien Nazis*... remember that time they marched out of their spaceship? I'll never forget it.

Imagine I drove you and some of our mutual friends to the movies. I accidentally left the child safety lock on, so you were trapped in the backseat and needed help opening your door. What is a fun and novel way to describe either the situation or my action? When this happened to one of my friends, he blurted out, "Oh, you have your car set on *kid prison mode!*" He took a potentially boring statement about a child safety lock and added a little extra flair and meaning to it by combining a few simple-but-normally-unassociated words.

The Mistaken Keyword

The source of a surprising number of laughs is when people mishear or misinterpret what someone has said. We've all done it—the difference between funny and not funny is how you react to the misunderstanding. For example, Dave was talking to Jenn about relationships.

> Jenn: I just want to find a guy who cooks and has a big couch so we can cuddle.
>
> Dave: Oh, I thought you said, 'big *POUCH*'! I was like, *Oh maybe you want him to carry you around in it like a baby kangaroo or something...* I thought that was weird, but I wasn't going to judge!

Did Dave really mishear Jenn? Maybe he did, and maybe he didn't. Maybe he did, and then realized what Jenn meant moments later, but decided to play up his mistake for fun anyway. Overly serious and Literal Larry wouldn't dare pretend like he misheard the word, because that doesn't make sense to someone so logical. Sometimes you should play for play's sake.

Homework

What's another way to say that you're *cold*? Or that something is *expensive*? Or that someone is *old*? Or *sick*? Or someone's beard is *messy*? Try to think of some ways yourself, and then read some example answers below when you're ready. (Hey! I saw you trying to skip ahead! Don't go any further until you think of some on your own).

> I think icicles are forming on my eyelashes.
>
> These wedding costs are starting to make my wallet cry.
>
> Isn't your hip replacement surgery coming up soon?
>
> My beard should be on a leash today.
>
> I felt like I had the plague mixed with a little scarlet fever.

Paint Better with Metaphors

Before you venture off on your quest to create colorful comments, pack some metaphors in your social backpack.

Real-life Example

The technical support guy at my work, let's call him Metaphor Mike, loves his metaphors. One time he was very tired and apologized. But instead of saying, "Sorry, I'm pretty tired," he playfully exclaimed, "Sorry, my brain is shutting down. I think my battery needs recharging."

One time, when I wanted the new operating system installed on my machine, but I asked to keep my old software, Mike answered, "Well you can't go halfway. You're either in the water or you're sitting on the beach getting a tan."

One time I made a mistake and Mike poked fun at me. He then followed it up with a fun metaphor, "I couldn't resist—you put the ball on a tee, and I took a swing at it!"

Why It Works

Metaphors (basically stating that one thing is another thing) aren't always funny on their own, but they often open the door to the play zone. And you know once the play zone is open, anything's possible. If you want people to joke around with you, you have to let them know that you're open to play. Figurative expressions (don't forget about clichés too) are like shortcuts to playful conversation.

I was in a meeting and someone stated, "I don't want to take us too far off the tracks." I remarked, "I think it's too late, we're already off the tracks and in a ditch somewhere." To which another colleague continued, "Yeah, a ditch in a remote part of Siberia, and I don't think we're finding our way back."

There are numerous ways you could phrase "going off the tracks" or off the road, or off the path. The metaphor could be a bus, a car, a train. Maybe John drove the bus and now it's hijacked by Jane. Maybe the bus crashed and the passengers are jumping out. The point is, regardless of the metaphor, it's often fun just to describe things in terms of other things. You never know who may latch on to your metaphor and add their own spin.

A joyful coworker once exclaimed, "I just finished my project so I can finally take it off the back burner!" To which someone added, "Now you just have to clear off the front burners and the microwave!"

Corporate buzzwords (and clichés in general) often get a bad rap, but they are popular for good reason; they are colorful and meaningful phrases packaged as a single soundbite. (I probably hear at least five buzzwords or clichés spoken every day at work.) There are endless opportunities to make fun of clichés, take them literally, or distort their meaning in some absurd way. Look at the following list of common buzzwords:

> It's the final *piece of the puzzle.*
>
> I'd like to take a *deeper dive* and see what we discover.
>
> I'm trying to *wrap my brain* around this whole thing.
>
> We can put that in *Jill's bucket* for now.
>
> Well, that *muddies the waters* a little.
>
> Why do I feel like I'm *walking into a minefield* here?
>
> Close? No, we're *still on the 50-yard line.*

Homework

Once a metaphor (or analogy or cliché) is introduced, see if you can twist, bend, and squeeze it into something else. Stretch it out like Silly Putty! How could you have even more fun with one of the aforementioned sports metaphors? Try to fill in the blanks:

I was trying to hit a home run, but I couldn't even _____.

I'd like to take a deeper dive, but we might discover _____.

I'm trying to wrap my brain around it but _____.

(*A few ideas:* 1. "...reach first base." 2. "...ten more projects waiting for us down below." 3. "...it's not rubbery enough to stretch that far.")

Technique #6

Exaggerate More or You'll Never Be Funny! Ever!

Humor loves exaggeration and wouldn't survive without it. Okay, maybe that's slightly hyperbolic, but exaggeration is the easiest, the best, the... just do it more. A lot more.

Real-life Example

Four people offer a comment about their strong coffee.

> Joe: This coffee might keep me up for *a while.*
>
> Pat: This coffee's going to keep me up *all night.*
>
> Justin: This coffee's going to keep me up *until next Tuesday!*
>
> Randal: This coffee's going to keep me up *until I'm 62.*

Why It Works

Of the four comments above, which is the *least* interesting? Most people would say Joe's comment. Can you see why? Could it be because Pat, Justin, and Randal all exaggerated the effects of the coffee? Of course! You may disagree, but I think Randal took it too far.

Everyday life isn't very exciting, but the key to funny exaggeration is to stay within the boundaries of reality, even if it's the very fringes (where TV stars get elected president of the United States). On occasion, going beyond the fringes works too, as long as it's still imaginable. Monty Python is famous for taking ideas to the extreme (e.g. killing a mosquito with a bazooka.) Good exaggerations often trigger quick mental visuals of the exaggerated event. If it's not remotely possible, people have difficulty suspending any disbelief. Coffee could certainly keep you up all night, and I suppose there could be a type of coffee that could keep you up multiple days. There's an art and science to good exaggerations, and in the coffee example, the best exaggerations live somewhere between Pat and Justin's comments.

One of the most alluring aspects of exaggeration is that it simply makes normal situations more interesting than they really are. Everyone knows and understands that the coffee won't keep anyone up for a week. You won't go to jail if you exaggerate. Western culture allows for such artistic license, and in fact, values and rewards it. Of course, you may want to refrain from exaggeration when your credibility is at stake.

Literal or factual comments will never be as visual, emotional, or dramatic as exaggerated comments. The next time you eat too much of Aunt Alice's BBQ pork or that giant bowl of Cincinnati chili, exaggerate the consequences. "I can barely move, I think someone's going to have to roll me back to work."

Describing your dad as "old" is boring. "Ancient" is better. Mentioning that he's so old, he "fought in the Civil War" is just plain fun! Check out the following simple exchange between Jen and Brian:

Jen: You don't like mushrooms on your pizza?

Brian: I never eat anything squishy and brown. It's my personal policy. And my secret to living so long!

Of course, Brian may eat squishy or brown things occasionally, but definitively stating that he never goes anywhere near anything even resembling a mushroom is entertaining.

Try exaggerating your own words or escalating someone else's to new levels. Simply describing something in a new or more exaggerated way commonly serves as a good response. Look at the progression of comments below:

Joe: I never knew he could make such a good sandwich.

Justin: That's because he's a sandwich visionary.

Randal: He's actually a culinary icon.

Pat: A global icon in the ham sandwich community.

Here's one more example describing sales in which each person builds on another's previous comment:

Joe: They're selling like hot cakes.

Justin: They're sweeping the nation.

Randal: They're going to turn this economy around!

Don't forget about *superlatives* (the biggest, the best, longest, etc.). Superlatives make everything more dramatic and interesting. Use them. Love them. Feel free to add some commentary after the superlative, also. For example, you're watching TV and observe, "He may have the *worst* serve in the history of men's tennis." While you're at it, follow up the superlative with an exaggerated example, "*Even my three-year-old nephew can hit the ball harder than that!*"

You're at an ice cream shop and they ask if you want one more scoop. A fun response? Try, "Sure, let's make it as gratuitous and fattening as possible!" This response also lends credence to the idea that you have an exaggerated appetite.

Exaggerated idiosyncrasies and quirks are usually very entertaining and should be taken advantage of. Maybe your hatred for cottage cheese causes you to feel ill just thinking about it (totally understood). Or maybe it causes you to become overly hostile and throw random objects. We all have pet peeves, some of us just react to them more violently than others.

Exaggerate the impact something has. Check out this interaction between two colleagues:

Catherine: Oh no, I spilled my water on your desk!

Mark: That's okay, it's not a big deal.

Nothing funny right? Right. Let's make Mark playfully exaggerate the impact of the incident this time.

Mark: *Great. You've completely ruined my desk.* Now I'm going to have to take the rest of the day off and find a new tree, chop it down, and build a new desk.

Do you smell that? A cooking example is coming. Stella baked a pumpkin pie, and then coincidentally, her friend Will stopped by soon after:

Stella: Hey good timing; want to try some pumpkin pie?

Will: Sure.

Nothing exaggerated or entertaining yet... but there's still hope! Suddenly Stella remembers this chapter:

Stella: I don't know if you know this, but I actually make the best pumpkin pie in all of Michigan.

Will: Oh yeah? Have you won any awards?

Stella: *A few.* I win the state pie contest every year. I actually plan to retire soon so other contestants get a chance.

Will: So, you're saying I have a chance to win it next year?

Are you starting to see how one exaggeration can ignite an explosion of playfulness? Not every exaggerated comment will take off, but they at least open the door to playfulness and create an opportunity for fun and humor.

Technique #7
React More Like a YouTuber

React more enthusiastically to the world around if you want to become more entertaining, engaging, and likable.

Real-life Example

One time I had to take my car in to have new tires put on. While waiting at the tire shop, I overheard a mechanic nearby exclaim in genuine astonishment, *"I have half a Butterfinger left! Awesome!* I completely forgot I left it there." All the other mechanics around him laughed.

Why It Works

In print, his remarks about the Butterfinger are nothing special. But the *way* he said it and the excitement he expressed at that moment is what evoked the laughter. No one laughed because he told a witty joke, or some entertaining story—all it took was acting overjoyed about discovering a half-eaten candy bar. (Exaggerating the impact of something so trivial is also part of what made it funny.)

I'm just going to say it: people who don't react much to anything are boring. Reacting isn't simply good for humor; it's good for simple engagement. If you haven't figured it out by now, engagement and humor go hand-in-hand. You can't make people laugh without being an active participant in the social situation; acting like a human statue doesn't cut it. React to what others say and do. React to your environment. Show some emotion.

In 2016, Candace Payne became famous for her reaction to a Chewbacca mask; you may better remember her as "Chewbacca

Mom." Her laugh and reaction were contagious, her video post immediately went viral, and she made millions of viewers smile and laugh seemingly overnight. (See link in the Recommend Viewing list at the end of the book.) There are now YouTube videos *reacting* to her *reaction*. She ended up doing the interview circuit, received book deals, and wrote a few books about laughter and joy—all because of one amazing reaction to a kid's mask. That's how powerful and captivating a good reaction can be.

I don't know Candace personally, but I bet she's the life of the party wherever she goes. You definitely don't need to achieve that level of zest and "joie de vivre" in order to be funny, but you can learn a lot from her.

Boring people react seriously and soberly to everything. Admittedly, I am not an excitable person by nature. That doesn't mean I don't possess just as many emotions as the next guy. If you react more like Darth Vader than Chewbacca Mom and don't naturally express emotion or feeling, you may want to consider acting a little until you get used to expressing yourself more colorfully. Yes, I'm saying act a little, if not for yourself, then for the sake of making the conversation experience more interesting and livelier for the other person.

Maybe your friend tells you they just returned from trying the menu at a new ice cream shop and it was delicious. If they are excited about it, try to reflect and share their energy. Don't bring down the mood with a somber "Cool." Share in their joy or excitement with a good reaction, "Really? I'm jealous! I wanted to try that place... what flavor did you get?" Celebrating or showing excitement over life's simple pleasures can be fun and set the stage for humor.

Have you ever witnessed relatives meeting a newborn baby for the first time? The rapid-fire succession of observations is amazing:

Oh, he's so sweet!

Look at his chubby little cheeks!

He's got such pudgy arms.

He's got Daddy's big brown eyes.

Look at that dark hair—she is definitely Jenny's baby.

Many poor conversationalists are very analytical and tend to sit and process information before reacting. Taking time to think through everything is a terrific strategy for those times when you need to buy stock or run a business, but by being too reflective and reticent you risk not sharing in the communal spontaneity and free-flowing nature of small talk.

Shane Dawson has made a killing just reacting on camera. He's created a variety of YouTube content, but one theme unifies nearly everything he's created: his reactions are entertaining. And he stands out from many others because he doesn't just react in dramatic fashion; he adds some entertaining commentary too. Just for fun, let's look at some of his comments as he reacts to tasting new food:

It tastes like something I've never had... like an entire garden.

You taste it first; I want to see if it stops your heart.

This looks like a dog toy... okay, it's too hard to bite. I've never had ice cream like that before.

These candies made me sick... and a little sad.

I just unintentionally made baby noises.

Whether or not he's your cup of tea, his videos have accumulated over 5 billion views. If he didn't react like that, he'd be broke, without any subscribers, and probably working as a barista in California somewhere. You don't have to react as melodramatically as Shane, but if you want more conversation "subscribers" (i.e., people who follow and listen to what you say), you should probably work on your reactions and observations.

Homework

If you aren't familiar with the Reaction Video genre, check out some other popular YouTube channels before reading further. *H3H3Productions*, *Reaction Time*, or *PaymoneyWubby* are wildly successful (unfortunately, some are mean-spirited). But even if you're not a fan, you can learn incredible lessons from them.

Knowing how to make interesting observations is the next important technique covered in this book and the funniest reaction-video YouTubers are masters at observational humor. They know how to look for and point out the ridiculous or interesting in the mundane—all without necessarily being exceptionally witty or clever. Study how they make observations. Your ability to engage people, maintain a fun conversation, and make people laugh will improve tenfold by engaging and reacting to the ordinary aspects of day-to-day life more dramatically.

Technique #8

Add Some Flavor to Your Opinion Soup

Everyone has opinions; make sure yours aren't boring.

Real-life Example

Read the following three bland opinions:

> I like M&M brownies a lot.

> I don't really like generic Q-tips.

> It doesn't come with cruise control? That's not good.

Let's take the same three opinions but add some strength and subjectivity to each one:

> I'm obsessed with M&M brownies; there's nothing better on this planet.

> I never go generic on Q-tips—there's only one Q-tip. The others are just wannabes. Generic brands are just little sticks that can poke out your eardrums.

> It doesn't come with cruise control? That's a deal breaker; if I can't cruise, I'm cruising out of here!

Why It Works

When you introduce more subjectivity, you start creating more interesting conversation and moving closer toward humor. For example, what if you see a naked statue in a garden, and you state "That's a naked statue." Good job, you just stated an objective fact.

However, you can push it further. Maybe you would call it R-rated? Then explain why it's R-rated. What is the impact on you or someone else? What should be done about it? Adding some more subjectivity and strength to the observation converts it into a more interesting opinion, which might sound more like:

> That's an R-rated statue—someone needs to get him some pants!

> Why are they keeping X-rated statues in a public park? Is this town being taken over by a bunch of nudist hippies?

> I think that once you become a statue you should be allowed to show any body part you want.

A rule of thumb is to save your stronger opinions for trivial topics so you mitigate the chance of offending someone. Because we know that humans are fascinated with superlatives, incorporate more hyperboles, categorical and absolute statements. *The Guinness Book of World Records* is popular for a reason.

Hey, speaking of Guinness, the beer drinkers out there will appreciate the following example. Imagine that you're at a friend's house and you spot a buddy drinking Guinness out of a can. If you're a beer connoisseur, you know *that's just wrong*. You have a few opinion options in this situation:

1) say nothing

2) say "I prefer my Guinness in a glass."

3) say "What are you doing? That's not a good idea."

But since this is a very trivial topic, why not take it up a notch? Option 4) could be "You can't drink Guinness out of a can, that's the worst way to drink it. In fact, that's treasonous. That's beer blasphemy! That's borderline criminal; you should be locked up in beer penitentiary." *Or something like that.*

Look at a few other examples:

I love it there; they have the *best* fitting rooms—the mirrors make me look so skinny!

That is the *worst* character on TV. Everything he does is illogical.

I still haven't tasted *anything more* delicious and grotesque than a cheesesteak from a street vendor at 2am.

That was the *wimpiest* moment of my life...

That was probably the *dumbest* thing I've ever done!

Playful opinions about other people and the nuances of human behavior constitute a large area ripe for exploring. For example:

He's supposed to be Elvis? I think my mother looks more like Elvis than that guy.

You turned into Wendy Williams on that one. I think you need to calm down.

I think you may have an addiction to chocolate-covered almonds. I know a good 12-step program if you need help.

Homework

Years ago, an elderly woman named Jean Hamilton, rose to fame for her signature catchphrase in ads for Frank's RedHot sauce. She always exclaimed at the end, "*I put that shit on everything!*" When it comes to opinions, be like Jean is with Frank's RedHot sauce. The fate of your humor relies on free-flowing information and viewpoints. Don't succumb to a passive mindset when it comes to offering opinions—be proactive and freely offer your thoughts and colorful observations (especially if they're non-offensive and about more trivial topics). Don't hold back your opinion or wait to be asked. Exaggerate. Dramatize. Have fun.

Check out YouTubers who review things. I enjoy *Shut Up & Sit Down* because they review board games in a very colorful way. They've mastered the art of describing *things*.

Technique #9
Stick a Label on It

By reducing complex things into simple categories or labels, your observations will often be funnier.

Real-life Example

> Randal: What do you guys drive?
>
> Fran: We drive a station wagon.

Fran's relying on a boring description. Come on, Fran, I think you can do better than that. Try a label, Fran.

> Fran: But it's so cheaply constructed; we call it our *plastic wagon.*

Much better Fran! Check out two people describing their personalities:

> Jen: I'm more of a hippy, crunchy, granola person.
>
> Brian: Yeah, well I'm more of a hunting-and-greasy-bacon kind of guy.

Why It Works

People love labels. And the best part is, you can stick them to nearly anything! Put something complex into an overly simplistic category and you'll probably spark some interesting or humorous conversation. Labels already come pre-loaded with meanings, memories, and feelings. You can even label actions or intentions.

If you pay attention, you'll notice labels everywhere. Read the following dialogue from the movie, *What About Bob* (Frank Oz, 1991):

> Dr. Marvin: Are you married?
>
> Bob: I'm divorced.
>
> Dr. Marvin: Would you like to talk about that?
>
> Bob: There are two types of people in this world: Those who like Neil Diamond, and those who don't. My ex-wife loves him.

Bob (played by the uniquely funny Bill Murray) leveraged a hilarious Neil Diamond label to simply describe his relationship.

Recently, I was listening to the radio on the way to work and the host of the show was talking about summer activities in Michigan. Read a summarized version of his transcript to see how he made the bit much more interesting:

> You can categorize 90% of my male listeners by one of three summer activities: There's *boat guy*, there's *golf guy*, and there's *cabin guy*. Boat guy spends his weekends waxing and fixing up his boat, and only ends up taking it out for four weekends before it gets too cold again. Then...

The radio host structured his entire afternoon show around those three labels. They worked well because they were also grounded in some truth. Callers to the show enjoyed discussing the intricacies of each lighthearted stereotype.

Make up new meanings for words or new words entirely. Do you walk up and down the stairs every day at work? Call it your "corporate aerobics." Does your daughter take care of visiting wildlife in the backyard? You could refer to her as the "Squirrel Whisperer." Holding the door open for someone at a party? Now you can playfully refer to yourself as your new role: "Bellhop," "Underpaid Doorman," or "Gatekeeper." Did your friend make fun of your cargo pants? Well they must have "pocket envy."

A teacher was complaining about teacher appreciation week. Instead of just saying she didn't like it, she said, "It's teacher appreciation week... but it should be called *shove donuts in your face week*."

Some friends walk by a classic cherry-red Lamborghini Countach.

> Kenny: You know they call it 'coontash' because apparently that's what people yell when it races by.
>
> Andy: And that's what I call any rich guy who's trying to show off by buying a Lamborghini. 'Look at that old *COONTASH* driving a Lamborghini!'

You're at a carnival. Your friend wants to ride the Tilt-a-Whirl, but you think it's too extreme. Instead of a boring "No," or "I can't handle that," you could state, "No way. It looks more like a Tilt-a-Hurl!"

If you (or someone else) add a successful label during a conversation, feel free to expand on it, explain why the label fits or does not fit, and so on. For example:

> Justin: You always have to keep everything don't you? You're such a *hoarder*.
>
> Melissa: I'm not a hoarder—I like to think of myself as a 'rescuer of trash.' I'm more *saver* than *hoarder*.

Generalize more. As long as you're making observations about trivial topics, it's okay to label and categorize indiscriminately.

Silly Human

Develop an eye for noticing subtleties in human behavior and appearance. Talk about the idiosyncrasies of the human condition.

Question why people act the way they do. Point out your own experiences and quirks. If you're feeling ambitious, reenact the behavior or mannerisms you've observed.

> That looks like your _____ (flirting / hungry / angry / bored) face.
>
> He gets that evil-villain wrinkle in his forehead—I don't know how he can make his face do that!
>
> Liam can't go a day without _____ (Coca-Cola / Donuts / checking his hair / etc.)

Don't miss out on opportunities to *mislabel* yourself or others in the name of comedy. For example, you could introduce Bryan to another friend, Mike (who happens to be outgoing and gregarious) and initiate with one of the following labels:

> This is Mike. He's incredibly aloof and unapproachable.
>
> This is Mike. He's pretty shy—I wouldn't try to engage him at all unless he makes eye contact with you first.

Make sure your label is blatantly wrong or someone may think there's some truth to it and be *confused* instead of *amused.*

Label Yourself

Don't forget about labels for yourself. Besides being safe, they're often funny.

> I feel like a *soccer mom*, except without the four kids, minivan, and dog.
>
> I don't want to sound like *get off my lawn* guy, but...
>
> I'm kind of a boss like that. Except for the fame and fortune part.

No one will sit next to me. Apparently, I repel people.

These are my fancy shoes. *Because I'm a fancy guy.*

I like Love Actually too. *Because I'm a romantic comedy kind of guy.*

Homework

How many labels can you think up for yourself?

Technique #10

That Looks Like...

Boost your observations and opinions even more by comparing things.

Real-life Example

Peggy and Larry are the stereotypical miserable middle-aged couple (the sick-of-each-other-but-too-lazy-and-broke-to-get-divorced kind). Here's a brief interaction:

> Peggy: Get your feet away from me!
>
> Larry: Why? They smell good.
>
> Peggy: No, they don't, they smell bad.

But that wasn't a particularly funny interaction, was it? Larry is going to sarcastically employ a comparison this time.

> Peggy: Get your feet away from me!
>
> Larry: Why? They smell like *freshly picked lilacs.*
>
> Peggy: Yeah right, if lilacs were left *rotting in a vase for five months!*

Someone call the fire department, because Larry just got burned! The simile encouraged Peggy to play along too, and the entire interaction became more fun and playful.

Why It Works

A friend once told me about a brand of razors I should purchase. He claimed the shaving experience was so smooth and effortless, it was "like a hot knife cutting through butter." I went out and purchased them that day. What he said was true. And that was over ten years ago, but I still think of his figurative example occasionally when I shave. Comparisons and analogies are powerful linguistic tools; tools that have been wielded by the greatest orators, comedians, politicians, salesmen, and conversationalists throughout all time. Compare more things. Be *like* Nike, and just do it. (See what I did there?)

As mentioned already (but just in case you weren't paying attention, I'll say it one more time), figurative language is usually more entertaining and enjoyable than literal language. Metaphor, simile, and other figurative language is your ticket to more colorful and imaginative commentary.

The statement "I feel like _____ right now" has limitless potential. You could fill in the blank with "a boy scout," "a loser," "I just got scammed," "a babysitter," or "waiter," etc. Keep in mind, as with many examples found in this book, some of these techniques only work when said with a smile or when it's obvious you're being facetious.

Here are some more similes to whet your fancy:

> He was so happy! He acted like he just won a million dollars.
>
> That looks like a 1970s shag carpet.
>
> Look at you with your notepad and pen—you're like a news reporter.
>
> We're all getting sick, except John, he's like an ox.
>
> It's becoming like *The Wild West* around here!
>
> He's like the guy who only calls when he needs something.

You may disclose: "I haven't gotten a pedicure in quite a while." But you could exaggerate the severity by saying: "It looks like a crime scene down there! CSI might be showing up soon."

You get into a friend's car on a hot day and notice his AC is barely working. Pointing out the issue, "Your AC seems like it's had better days..." is a good segue to a label or simile: "It feels kind of like a tiny Eskimo is breathing on my legs. It's not very cold, but it's still better than nothing."

I overheard a hilarious simile about how women have it easy when it comes to finding dates through dating apps and websites. The conversation went something like the following:

> Bob: Women have it much easier than men when it comes to dating apps. For women it's like fishing with dynamite. For me, it's like there are only four fish in the lake and 1,000 other guys fishing that day.
>
> Larry: ...and you're fly fishing.
>
> Bob: ...and it's your first time trying to fly fish.
>
> Larry: ...and you keep hitting yourself in the face.

Notice how Larry and Bob were both able to continue to play with the simile after it was introduced?

Homework

Let's practice by looking at some more Peggy and Larry interactions, shall we?

> Larry: You like gingerbread coffee too?
>
> Peggy: Yeah, I do. It's good.

Instead of remarking that the gingerbread coffee is "good," how else could she describe it? What does gingerbread coffee remind you of? Let's try it again.

> Larry: You like gingerbread coffee too?
>
> Peggy: Yeah, I do. It's like a little piece of Christmas in a cup.

Much better Peggy! Let's try another one.

Larry: The hotel breakfast looks cheap.

Peggy: You're right, it doesn't look very good.

This time, what's another way Peggy could describe something looking cheap? What would a bunch of old food sitting out on a table remind you of? Maybe old items sitting out at a garage sale? Check out the new interaction:

Larry: The hotel breakfast looks cheap.

Peggy: You're right, it looks more like a *breakfast garage sale*. The coffee machine looks like it's been sitting in someone's attic until this morning.

Much better! Adding figurative language dramatically transforms each interaction into a more entertaining experience. Drawing the connection between two seemingly unrelated things—like breakfast and a garage sale, is a key part of why it works.

Section 3

Imagine

Technique #11

You "Could" Master the Hypothetical Comment

A single hypothetical statement could launch a boring conversation into a world of fictional, hilarious fun.

Real-life Example

I was sitting in a coffee shop while writing this book, when a large middle-aged man came over and asked if the comfy chair next to me was available. I gave him my standard polite head nod and a "Yep." He sat down, got comfortable, rested his head against the back of the comfy seat, and stated, "If I start snoring loudly, just kick me."

We both laughed. I responded, "I've got some ice left in my cup I could pour on you if that's better than kicking you." He laughed again, and I went about my work. Either of us could have continued a conversation very naturally from there if we had wanted, all because of an unlikely imaginary event—falling asleep and snoring in a coffee shop chair!

Why It Works

What if I told you that some of the best and funniest conversation exchanges are about things that never occurred and never will? Hypotheticals are probably the most entertaining types of statements in the entire conversation universe. Funny people everywhere rely on them. For example, there was nothing glamorous about the aforementioned snoring in the chair event, but simply discussing the hypothetical possibility, within the context of a coffee shop, was funny and resulted in instant laughter. We're humans; most of us have active imaginations and like to ponder what could be. We like to imagine ourselves or others in different situations.

Let's review a simple, boring interaction. You're tired and say to your colleague, "I'm so tired."

Now let's see how a hypothetical could spice it up a bit: "I'm so tired. Do you think it would look bad if I slept under my desk for a few minutes?" Much better!

Let's look at another simple workplace example. Your friend Carole is washing her cup in the communal sink at work. She notices you approaching and says, "Hold on, I'll move over."

What was so funny about that? That's right, nothing. In real life, Carole proceeded to add a hypothetical and it resulted in a funny interaction. She said, "Hold on, I'll move over. I don't want to get soap all over your suit. *Then everyone would know for a fact that I'm a klutz!*"

Let's look at some quick examples *without* and *with* a hypothetical component. Obviously, you weren't privy to the actual conversations, but my hope is you can imagine how B-O-R-I-N-G some of these statements are *without* hypotheticals compared to the versions *with* hypotheticals.

Without hypothetical: I love Laffy Taffy.

With hypothetical: I love Laffy Taffy. *I would eat a whole bag right now if I saw one!*

Without hypothetical: Yeah, I was going to call you this morning to see if you were coming in.

With hypothetical: Yeah, I was going to call you this morning to see if you were coming in. *I wanted to make sure you weren't stranded in a ditch off I-75 somewhere.*

Without hypothetical: I have to go give that presentation now.

With hypothetical: I have to go give that presentation now. *Anyone want to come see me embarrass myself?*

Without hypothetical:

Jack: I'm so glad they're finally building a Bob's Burger down here.

Jill: Yeah.

With hypothetical:

Jack: I'm so glad they're finally building a Bob's Burger down here.

Jill: Yeah, but *I'll probably gain about twenty pounds!*

How many times have you met someone, and responded with something like, "John? Nice to meet you." Probably hundreds, right? Next time, add a little hypothetical:

John? Nice to meet you. I'm so bad with names; I'll probably have to ask for your name at least three more times today!

If you're feeling extra playful, try an even better version of the line that gets a chuckle every time I try it:

John? Nice to meet you. I'm so horrible with remembering names; I'll probably call you Tony or Steve at some point, but I'll eventually get it right!

Hypothetical comments sometimes exaggerate what could, would, or should happen in the future. Sometimes they reference what could have occurred in the past. Not surprisingly, hypotheticals require a playful audience or environment or else they'll fall flat. Here are a few more examples to get the fun wheels turning:

> Your beard's becoming epic. I think you should shave lightning bolts into it before your next marathon—it would help you run faster.

> Since nobody likes me anymore, I'm just going to retire early and move to the Bahamas.

> I've always wanted to have a home brewery in my basement. That would be so cool! Except I'd probably end up gaining 25 pounds!

> It should be against the law to serve onions at work—my breath is poisonous right now!

> I love that song! I think that song should be played every time I walk into my office. Can you make that happen, please?

Some hypotheticals involve talking about what things would be like under a different circumstance, with different people, or maybe even in a parallel dimension. Rearranging reality, even for a moment, can be great fun.

For example, your friend doesn't have change for the drink he asked you to buy for him. You could say something boring, or you could say something playful like, "You know, if I were a mob boss, you'd be shot in the kneecaps for pulling something like that." The example essentially follows this structure:

This isn't/We aren't/I am not _____, but if it/we were/I was
_____, then _____ would/wouldn't happen.

Homework

Why do I have a habit of dumping a ton of examples on you throughout this book? It's because part of the process of rewiring your neurons and learning new conversational habits requires reading, listening, and trying new comments. When you come across a list like the one I included in this chapter, I suggest reading the examples aloud multiple times. Train your brain to start using hypothetical phrases. Read them over and over. Try to practice them as much as possible. Restate in your own words and develop your own comedic style. You *should* start dreaming of hypothetical statements in your sleep.

Technique #12

You "Should" Understand the Parts of the Hypothetical

There are many reasons why a hypothetical is successful; make sure you understand them all.

Real-life Example

> Think about what you'd be doing, like, 40 years ago, you know. Think about what that would be like. What you'd be doing, like, on a Thursday night. You know, you're just sitting in your house, by yourself... you're in a wooden chair... eating a can of beans.

Why It Works

That's an excerpt from an Aziz Ansari performance in front of thousands of people at Madison Square Garden. But the Aziz excerpt doesn't seem that funny does it? He actually made his massive audience laugh with the last few lines about the wooden chair and can of beans. Before continuing, I strongly suggest you watch it right now if you're able. On second thought, you're not allowed to continue reading until you do. I'm not joking. (See Recommend Viewing at the end of the book for the link if you can't find it by searching.)

Why did it get laughs? For three main reasons:

1. He delivered it with great enthusiasm and good timing
2. He included a few key details—wooden chair and can of beans
3. The entire segment was a relatable hypothetical

We can all learn from Aziz the steps to make people laugh. Deliver with more enthusiasm, check. Add a few key details, check. And lastly, use more relatable hypotheticals, check.

As mentioned earlier, offering too many details can be boring and time-consuming, but a lack of details can be dull, too. Find the perfect balance by including a few key details in most of your comments. Aziz didn't just say "chair," he said, "wooden chair." That's twice as visually interesting to imagine. He painted a quick mental picture. Aziz could have replaced the can of beans with a stale box of Cheerios, or a can of tomato soup, and he would have achieved the same laughter.

Start Strong

Hypotheticals don't have to be as long and drawn out as the example Aziz delivered. Some are short and quick. Additionally, start with an exaggerated statement because it's safer than going straight into a hypothetical statement without any context.

The following hypothetical statements are each preceded by an exaggerated statement (*italicized*) that sets up the topic and the line of thought:

> *I think my dog hates me*—so I'm going to let him have the house and I'll find someplace new to live.

> *You'd be embarrassed to watch me play softball*—I'd probably break both my ankles during the first game. I'd be out for the season.

Initiate with definitive or categorical statements, and the hypotheticals may naturally follow as support for the initial statement. Let's break down a few examples, shall we?

Liam: Is your son talking a lot yet?

Henry: Oh yeah, *he won't shut up!*

Henry set up the context with a strong exaggerated description of his son, so a hypothetical could slide right in as support for his first comment.

> Henry: ...Sometimes I just want to keep shoving chips and candy bars in his mouth, just so I could get five minutes of silence!

Here's another one where Melissa discusses her husband Justin's sleeping habits: "Justin's a great sleeper... nothing could wake him up!" Melissa introduced a hyperbolic statement, so the opportunity is ripe for some hypothetical follow-up statements:

> Melissa: There could be construction going on in the next room. Someone could be jackhammering our tile floor and he would keep sleeping!

Have you ever been bombarded with questions before? In that scenario, you could respond with a strong assertion, "You guys are asking like 1,000 questions!" Once the stage is set, it's ripe for a hypothetical to support your assertion. For example:

> What is this, some kind of intervention?
>
> I feel like I'm being interrogated right now. Are you about to bust out a lie detector test, too?
>
> Are you both working for the FBI?
>
> I feel like I'm in a therapy session right now... where's a couch I can lie down on?

I'm dangerously close to including too many examples in this chapter, but the following was so good I couldn't leave it out! My colleague, Sheila, was celebrating her birthday at work and her present from us was buried in a bag full of colored paper stuffing. Notice how she started with a strong observation:

Sheila: Wow, there's a ton of paper in here; *I mean a ton!*

The stage was set up for funnier comments. She supported her initial assertion with a sarcastic hypothetical.

Sheila: *Did you buy every piece of paper in the store?* Do they have any left?

She followed it up with another hypothetical a few seconds later. She pulled off a difficult but hilarious double hypothetical combo.

Sheila: I don't know if I'll ever find the gift! I might need a break soon!

Remember, start with a strong, exaggerated opinion and the hypothetical comments will more naturally and easily follow.

The popular online social platform, Reddit is full of these types of discussions where one person introduces a categorical opinion that triggers an avalanche of hypothetical examples. It's easy to find Reddit comments like, "I think I'd rather have anyone else in the world be President than Trump." Once the hypothetical is setup, the possibilities are endless. For example, other people may chime in with responses like, "I'd prefer Bernie Sanders, Chelsea Clinton, or even Barack Obama's dog, Bo." Assuming you're not a Trump fan, what other options would you rather have running the country? How far could you push it? How about:

Daenerys Targaryen

A glass of Chardonnay

An inflatable couch

Vincent Price's ghost

A bull shark

That woman who keeps robocalling my cell phone and leaving messages in Mandarin

A vintage Teenage Mutant Ninja Turtles action figure

That container that's been in the back of the breakroom fridge so long, no one can tell what it actually was. Maybe refried beans?

Make Your Hypotheticals Relevant and Relatable

Your hypothetical statements should connect to the current situation or involve people and things that are relevant to the people in your social groups. For example, Saturday Night Live comedians love to mock politicians in the news. One time, I showed someone a recent SNL skit, and the person didn't get it. There was no laugher, just confusion. Cue the classic advice: "Know your audience."

By inserting yourself or familiar people into the hypothetical, you'll naturally keep the topic more relevant (and more likely to be funny) to everyone in the conversation. Check out the example below where Erin inserts herself into a hypothetical scenario.

In the following interaction, some friends discuss the topic of women who choose to become surrogate mothers for money.

Sam: Who would want to be a surrogate just for money?

Maureen: My cousin did it. She made nearly $30,000!

Erin: Maybe I should do it! I could quit my job, just grow babies every year and retire when I'm 45.

Sam: What would you tell people?

Erin: I'm a *professional baby-maker.*

Maureen: Yeah! You could have a business card with a smiling fetus on it.

Erin: I would just sit around and eat ice cream all day! I think I could handle that!

A few friends discuss an article one of them read about Japanese culture. Notice how Mike and Abe insert themselves into the hypothetical situation in different ways.

Mark: Have you heard about that new company in Japan that pays men to listen? Women pay hundreds an hour to go on 'listening dates.'

Mike: How much do they pay again? And where can I sign up? I'll start tomorrow.

Abe: You couldn't pay me enough for that job! I would quit after five minutes.

Mark: I think a requirement is that you could cry on demand, just in case she tells a sob story.

Mike: Okay, then I'm definitely out. I'm not a crier.

Hypothetical Statements Usually Involve Activity

Hypothetical statements often involve something happening or something changing. You don't have to be an active person, but you should aim for more activity-based statements. These types of statements won't always be funny, per se, but they are at least interesting. And that's a good start.

I was recently telling a friend about the time my wife and I forgot to pay a toll road in Illinois and six months later received a bill for $750! My friend shared my outrage over the incident and exclaimed, "For that much money, they should name the entire highway after you! You should never have to pay another toll again!" Check out some additional action-oriented examples:

> I'm thinking about eating this entire pie right now—I mean, how bad would that really be?

> That goat is friendly, can I take him with me? I need a goat in my life.

> I think you should go talk to her... she keeps looking at you. Or maybe she's just a creeper. Hard to tell. You should go find out though.

> Everyone please write what you're bringing to the potluck on the wall... *If you don't, I'll come hunt you down. I know where you work.*

Make Mismatch Connections

Much of comedy, and most certainly hypothetical comments, often depend on drawing connections between seemingly incongruous or unrelated things.

Recently, a Game of Thrones episode aired, in which a cast member accidently left a Starbucks cup in one of the scenes next to Daenerys Targaryen (the heroine in the medieval drama series). Now don't get me wrong, that mismatch itself is comedic, but it opened the door to additional lighthearted connections. If it's true that someone left a Starbucks cup, what else could be true about the situation? It helps to think about any well-known facts or perceptions about Starbucks. I'll give you the answer: Starbucks employees are known for misspelling names on cups. So when talking about the Starbucks incident with friends, a connection could be made, for example, like the following: "Her name was probably misspelled as Daenielle." Or "Denise Tangerine."

Recently, there was a news report that referenced a new study claiming that bed bugs actually arrived around the time of the dinosaurs. One of the keywords in that statement is *bed bugs*. What else in our world is generally understood to have bed bugs? Think of anything? I don't know about you, but I immediately think of a lot of hotels and motels. For the sake of not offending any actual hotel or motel chains, let's make up a hotel company called Best Sleep. A connection could be made here that sounds like, "Coincidentally, that's also when Best Sleeps first opened up." The connection isn't openly stated, but the meaning is understood and humor is the byproduct.

Start looking for more connections between seemingly disparate things and see if you can spark a little humor.

It's Hypothetical Time

Need help thinking of hypotheticals? Think about your *timeline*: what could have happened in the past, what would you do immediately, or what might you do in the near future? Notice the following example applies all three directions of time.

You're at a conference, and someone is telling everyone at your table about a brand-new amazing app that can change how we use healthcare. Everyone is impressed, and all you can muster is, "That's so cool."

If you were thinking about your timeline, you may have offered one of the following comments:

PAST

That's great. Now I'm thinking maybe I should have bought a new phone instead of that goat yoga class.

PRESENT

That's so cool! I'm going to go home and tell my husband. He'll be shocked that I know something about healthcare technology before he does!

FUTURE

So, does this mean that I won't have to see a doctor anymore? Because I'm all for that!

Homework

Let's practice. Below are some classic hypothetical phrase structures. Can you think of a few words to fill in the blanks? There are no right or wrong answers—just get your brain used to making these types of comments.

> I'm horrible/great at _____. If I did _____, then _____ would happen.
>
> I can't stand _____. If _____ one more time, I will _____.
>
> I love/I'm obsessed with _____. If _____, then _____.
>
> That was horrible! They would have been better off if they just _____.
>
> Why would he/she/they do that? He/she/they could have at least _____.

Technique #13

Imagine the Impact

You'll have an easier time thinking of hypothetical comments if you consider the playful consequences of everyday things.

Real-life Example

> Children: What are we eating tonight?
>
> Mother: Daddy's cooking dinner this time... *so it may or may not be edible.*

> Dave: We should play basketball sometime.
>
> Kenny: I don't think you'd like that... *I may make you cry in front of your wife and kids.*

Go back and read the above examples again, but this time stop before the italicized parts. They're not as entertaining, are they? You probably figured out that the italicized words are the hypothetical parts—the potential consequences of some event occurring.

Why It Works

We've already discussed how important hypotheticals are to conversational humor. You'll have an easier time thinking of hypothetical statements if you're always considering hypothetical consequences or playful outcomes.

Talk about the potential impact some action or comment has on you, someone or something else. Talk about how someone else might feel—how might someone else react? How would their action or behavior change as a result? What would change once the event does or doesn't take place? What would have happened if the event already occurred? Let's look:

> Mark: My daughter got invited to join the premier soccer league this summer.
>
> Jason: That's great news.

Nothing too interesting yet. But then Jason decides to exaggerate the impact that event might have. Andy and Mark play along and continue the fun.

> Jason: ...you'll be doing a lot of traveling though. This is the beginning of the end. We might never see you again.
>
> Andy: Next thing you know, his daughter's getting a full ride to some Euro league, she's dominating the Euro circuit, and Mark's living in some little Villa in the south of France.
>
> Mark: Hey, well I'd definitely let you guys stay with me... the first bottle of wine's on me!

Consider a few more examples:

> Maureen: I didn't shave my legs for nearly three months during that trip... I know, sexy huh?
>
> Libby: Oh yeah! *I bet your husband loved it!* Is he into the furry leg thing?
>
> Maureen: Hey, some guys are into the *orangutan legs.*

Sue: I needed to throw out the whiteboard. It was falling apart.

Patrick: You did? Kim's not going to be happy; she loved that thing. When she gets in tomorrow, she's most likely going to throw her fake Peace lily plant at you.

Sue: You're probably right, but I always wanted a fake Peace lily plant, so that would actually work out well.

Notice in the previous example, Patrick could have said that Kim would throw "something" generic at Sue. But instead, he leveraged a fun, relevant detail (Peace lily plant) which helped spark the imagination a little more. Sue was able to play along better because she pounced on his extra detail about the Peace lily.

Dialogue

"Dialogue makes everything better!" shouted Greg just now. Dialogue not only helps your hypotheticals come to life, but it also opens another outlet for artistic freedom and chance to engage your listener. Exaggerate how the characters in your hypotheticals react. Embellish the impact some event has on the people in your story. Ang introduces a hypothetical:

Ang: I'm hoping that Timmy goes to the bathroom soon because if he doesn't, he's going to be cranky for the entire flight!

Ang could expand on her own hypothetical by discussing the impact it would have on herself or others and what someone may say or think. For example:

And: I would be so embarrassed! Other passengers are going to be like, 'Control your kid, lady!'

Check out a few more:

Susan: How many shoes do you own?

Tom: If you ever saw my collection, you wouldn't believe it belonged to one man. You'd probably say, 'That's too many shoes for one person to wear! *That's impossible!*'

Geoff: It'll be fine.

Maureen: Watch, it's totally not going to work and he's going to walk in and be like, '*What's wrong with you people!?*'

It's fun to talk about what could, should or would happen, but don't forget to talk about what *wouldn't ever* happen, too. This example also includes good dialogue.

I don't do well at bars anymore since I gained weight. It's not like a girl's going to look at me from across the bar and say to herself, 'Oh, he has the perfect beer belly... I haven't seen one of those in years.'

Technique #14

Imagine a Playful Explanation

You can think of more hypotheticals if you explore explanations for why something exists or occurred.

Real-life Example

I was leaving a neighborhood party when my neighbor commented about my five-year-old.

> Neighbor: Your son has been so good this whole time.
>
> Me: Thanks. It worked out well.

The conversation could end there. But it didn't. I added a playful reason as to why my son behaved so well.

> Me: Thanks! We got lucky. Someone probably snuck him a few beers from the fridge!

Why It Works

It should be clear by now—hypothetical comments are awesome. Adding a playful explanation for something is just another way to incorporate that sweet, sweet hypothetical magic into your conversations.

Looking back on the chapter's opening example, it can be funny to imagine for a moment that someone slipped a crazy kid some beer just to get him to calm down. It's not something that would actually happen (at least, not where I'm from!), so it's a hypothetical that exists in a potentially fun, but safe zone. Hypothetical explanations that dive into death and disease and blood and guts are not recommended for most audiences, so the key is to find the edgy-but-safe zones.

Your audience may get offended instead of amused if you don't correctly gauge what their tolerance is for hypothetical scenarios. You could have tamed this scenario down by saying that someone slipped him a Nyquil instead of a few beers. You, the reader, could have been offended by the beer example—I took a risk even including it. Of course, there are numerous ways someone could have calmed a child down; it's up to you to figure out which reason works for your audience in that particular situation. You won't always know of course, but you should have an idea. If you're absolutely clueless as to how they'd react, here's a tip: don't try it at all.

Similar to other types of hypotheticals, hypothetical explanations require a good amount of imagination. Let's look at some more examples.

Some friends talk about hair loss.

> Joe: Yeah, it sucks, I'm sure I'll be bald in about two years.
>
> Justin: Really, you look like you still have all your hair.

Joe could confirm that he does, or he could offer a playful explanation first.

> Joe: That's because I'm wearing a toupee, a really good one. In fact, I just glued it down this morning.

Two friends are talking about the United States men's national soccer team.

> Ben: I don't get it. How could they lose to Iceland so easily? The U.S. has like 30 times the population.
>
> Blake: It's because the Iceland players practice on ice all year round, except for when they play in the World Cup. That's why they have such an advantage.

Mike told Mark that his dog puked on the rug. Mark responds with a normal opinion.

Mark: You might want to get him checked out.

But Mark lightens up the conversation even more by offering a hypothetical explanation.

Mark: Maybe you shouldn't feed him cheese and whiskey for breakfast!

Some friends talk about a minor health concern.

Maureen: My hands feel like they're too cold. Maybe I should go see my doctor.

Tom: It's no big deal.

Tom offers a playful reason as to why he's so confident.

Tom: I'm sure nothing's wrong with you. I watch Grey's Anatomy every season, so I'm basically a doctor now.

Some friends drive through a small town.

Andy: Who would name a town 'Sebewaing?' What a silly name.

Kenny: I think it's Native American for 'I'm sorry.' Like if one Native American accidentally steps on another one's tepee and knocks it over, he yells, 'Oh no, Sebewaing! Sebewaing!'

Andy: Well *I'm sorry* for making us drive through this boring town.

Homework

You chat with a co-worker about how their meeting went the week before.

> Co-worker: The meeting didn't go as I hoped. I don't think they liked my proposal.
>
> You: That's too bad.

What else could have been the reason for the poor presentation? You could add a playful hypothetical explanation to lighten up the mood. Can you think of something? Obviously, you don't have the entire context, but try to think of something before continuing and get your brain used to coming up with more hypotheticals. Here's what was actually said:

> You: Maybe you shouldn't have worn your ugly Christmas sweater to the meeting. It probably didn't make a good impression.
>
> Co-worker: You're right—you don't think they liked the big picture of Rudolph on the front? Or the blinking lights?

The more you know about another person, the more you can tailor your hypotheticals to what they'd enjoy. What's something they may have possibly done? Are they known for being obsessed with their dog, Lila? Maybe they accidentally left photos of their dog in the presentation? Anyway, you get the idea.

Technique #15
Talk About the Almost

An easy way to incorporate more hypotheticals is to talk about what almost occurred.

Real-life Example

> Joyce: How'd the event go?
>
> Jay: It was fun... yeah, it was good for the most part.

Jay missed an opportunity to mention what *almost* happened. The "almost" moments are sometimes more interesting because they open the door to playful hypothetical possibilities. Try again, Jay.

> Jay: It was fun... *the tent almost collapsed*, but other than that, it was a good time.
>
> Joyce: The tent almost collapsed? Oh no! How'd that happen?
>
> Jay: Well, funny story...

Why It Works

Often in life, someone will inquire about the outcome of some event. The problem is, events are often *uneventful!* Here is where this technique shines. Even if the event was boring, you can still add a hypothetical referencing what *didn't* quite happen or what *almost* happened.

At my son's 6th birthday party, I almost forgot to fill the piñata with candy. One of my friends, Erin, was astonished at such an oversight and initiated the "almost" hypothetical statement for me.

> Erin: You almost forgot? Oh, my gosh! You almost had a total party crisis on your hands. You almost had ten crying kids!

Everyone laughed. My friend and I continued the hypothetical about what *almost* happened.

> Me: I know—that would have been the worst piñata ever! The kids would have been so confused.
>
> Erin: We could say, 'Well, this is one of those new healthy piñatas. Instead of candy... it gives you exercise.'

Want to upgrade your stories and observations? Try to insert more "almost" comments. Check out some examples:

> Then he did it again... *I almost threw the money back on the table and walked out,* but...
>
> *And I wanted to run over there and kick him in the face,* but I decided that I'm too civilized to do that.
>
> I was so close to *just leaning over and giving him a big fat kiss on the lips.*
>
> *I almost told him to 'go jump off a cliff,'* but I figured he'd probably fire me for saying that, so I decided not to.
>
> *I almost fainted,* but then I remembered it was all fake...

I was listening to someone tell the following story about a scary moment from childhood:

> For my birthday, we rented one of those inflatable bounce castles. Well, after the parents went inside, it started to collapse... my cousin started to freak out because her hair got trapped in the net part and she was slowly getting sucked under this thing. *I literally thought she was going to die under a deflated castle!*

That last line about fearing the worst outcome for her cousin is what sparked the laughter. Her cousin was never in any real danger, but the fact that she thought that something terrible almost happened was the funny part. In retelling, she knew that nothing bad had happened, so she used a dramatic/comedic voice to exaggerate the fear. Don't neglect the role that the delivery's tone and nonverbal can have in intensifying the effect.

Technique #16
Seek Hypothetical Solutions
Is there a problem? What's a hypothetical solution to the problem? Do you wish something was better? Conversely, what if something was worse? How much worse could it get?

Real-life Example

> Fran: My husband is getting worried about losing all his hair.
>
> Randal: So am I! I don't have many good hair years left.
>
> Joe: I think we should bring back the powdered wig. *That would solve so many problems for men!*
>
> Randal: That would be great. The 1700s knew what they were doing.

Why It Works

The benefit of talking about a *problem* (especially a lighthearted one), is that it opens the door to hypothetical *solutions* to the problem.

When my wife Maureen and I were first married, we moved to a new house. One night, my wife saw kids in costumes walking by our house. Maureen yelled to me, "We forgot to get any candy! What are we supposed to do if they ring our doorbell?" We had totally forgotten that our city sometimes does Halloween on a different night, and we weren't prepared. I yelled back a funny solution based on what we had in the house, "We should just hand out chicken strips and green beans." She played along with other hypothetical solutions, like, "I have some of grandma's old toys in the garage." We had a few laughs imagining those ideas playing out. I finally concluded, "We'll never have trick-or-treaters again."

On a different evening, my wife and I finished watching a movie and my wife commented, "That movie had such a sad ending... I wasn't prepared for that." Did you notice her statement contained a problem? Sometimes they're subtle. My solution? "They should put a warning label on that movie! Like *'Warning, your favorite character will most likely die a horrible death.'*"

Remember, think about what you or someone else could/should do if money / time / education / health / law / morals / physics was not an issue. Stretch your imagination. Let's look at some more examples:

Three people are waiting for coffee at work. Anya offers a simple observation.

> Anya: Looks like everyone's waiting for coffee.

> Kaerigan: Yeah, there's even a line forming.

Kaerigan exaggerated the situation slightly. Nothing too interesting has been said yet, but a small problem has been introduced. Someone should solve the problem with a hypothetical solution!

> Rowan: We're going to have to get one of those rope barriers like at the movies to keep the crowds under control.

Problem solved! (hypothetically, of course) Good job, Rowan.

Rick meets up with his friends and starts a conversation around his latest problem.

> Rick: I totally got lost in the parking garage there. It took almost 20 minutes to get out. All the floors look the same.

Someone needs to offer Rick a hypothetical solution to his problem.

Lincoln: I think they should give the sections better names—numbers and letters are useless.

Rick: You're right, they should try more creative names like 'Hey Jerk Face' ... or 'I'm so hungry!' How could you forget that? You'd never get lost again!

Jen's friend Paula is five months pregnant. Jen is growing impatient and expresses how she wants to see the baby sooner. This made-up problem—that the baby is taking too long—sets up a hypothetical solution.

Jen: I can't wait to see your baby! I think you should just have the baby now. Would you be okay with that?

Paula: Well if you really can't wait any longer, I guess I could look into it. I mean, who cares if it would be incredibly bad for my baby.

Jen: Great. I know a guy who might do the surgery for you.

Paula: I bet. Does he live in the alley behind your house?

Jen: Yes! How did you guess? He said he'd do it for only $20, too. I can probably get you a coupon online.

See how a hypothetical solution can launch an entire cavalcade of hypothetical play? Of course, it takes the right social setting and partner to really take off, but when it does, it's pure social joy.

It's winter, Jon and Matt are walking to the store, and pass a dirty-looking snowman. It just takes one observation about a hypothetical problem for hilarity to ensue.

Jon: That's the saddest looking snowman I've ever seen.

Matt: He looks a little disheveled.

Jon: He could use some makeup or something.

Matt: He could probably use a bath. He's kind of dirty.

Jon: But then his face would melt off, he can't do that.

Matt: But how's he supposed to pick up snowgirls looking all messed up like that?

Jon: I think he's consumed too much eggnog... he's a little fat around the mid-section.

Matt: Yeah, he definitely needs to cut back on the nog. Maybe just stick to carrots.

Jon: No, he can't do that. Then he'd be eating his own nose. We don't want cannibal snowmen around here.

Matt: You're right, what was I thinking?

What if no problems are immediately evident? Sometimes, the solution is already present and you need to come up with a hypothetical problem. For example:

You're at an Easter party and the kids are picking up Easter eggs at a frantic pace. Everything's going smoothly.

Dave: It's too bad we can't get them to pick up their toys with that much enthusiasm.

Michelle: I wish we could rent them out to local cities for trash pickup. Think of the money we'd make!

Another twist on this technique is to consider what would make something much worse.

Lisa: What should we order for lunch?

Erin: I don't care, I'll eat anything... except for mushrooms.

Lisa: Oh yeah? Because I was thinking we could just go pick some morels in the field over there and have a picnic.

Lisa quickly thought of the worst possible hypothetical solution to the problem and it resulted in a few laughs. Note that including the extra detail (e.g., morels) was what helped take this hypothetical to the next level.

Homework

> Liam: I tried to buy the new Venom DVD, and they don't accept American Express. I had to give it back. I was so mad.
>
> Caitlin: Really? They don't take Amex? That's crazy.
>
> Liam: Could you do me a favor and call up their CEO and explain my story? I don't know who he is, but I bet he'd understand.
>
> Caitlin: You think he might be a big Venom fan?
>
> Liam: Oh yeah, I mean, who isn't?

Think about a situation where you weren't pleased with a company policy or service. Fixing the problem by saying you're going to call (or asking your friend to call) the CEO is funny because it's such an extreme solution. Obviously, you'd never call a CEO, and probably couldn't do that, but it's fun to think through what would happen if you did. Maybe you could exaggerate further and talk through how you're going to kidnap the CEO's dog until he listens to your demands... *because I'm sure that would go well.* What's an outrageous solution for a problem you've encountered recently?

Section 4

Entertain

Hit 'em with the Right Hook

Entertaining articles, stories and songs usually have a hook designed to grab peoples' attention. Interesting and funny comments are no different.

Real-life Example

> Liam: What are you doing this weekend?

> Caitlin: Well, my boyfriend is coming over to my house.

There's nothing wrong with the factual response, however, it's missing the interesting parts: Caitlin forgot to mention that this is the *first time* her boyfriend is meeting her son. That's much more likely to hook someone in. That's the more interesting narrative. Along those lines, she could have added: "And I'm really nervous! He's never met my son. I hope my son doesn't do anything crazy!"

Another possible hook could have been: "And I'm torn about what we're going to do—I mean, my son hates sports and my boyfriend is the biggest sports fanatic and wants to watch the game."

Why It Works

You'll stand a better chance of hooking someone into your stories and observations when there's an interesting angle. And I'm not talking about acute vs. obtuse either. A good angle introduces drama or intrigue into the story and is often what hooks someone in. Interesting angles consider unique perspectives or compelling viewpoints. In the previous example, once Caitlin confessed that it was the first time her boyfriend was meeting her son, she introduced drama and suspense into the conversation. Would the son behave? What crazy thing might the son do? Would the boyfriend react a certain way? How could this drama be exaggerated and made even more playful?

Let's step back for a moment. At a high-level, the majority of conversation is based around exchanging information. Person A: "Did you eat lunch?" Person B: "Yes, I did." Subpar conversationalists lean heavily on factual, literal comments too often and forget the fun, figurative, emotional human stuff. As you process information, start looking for interesting narratives to pull out of it. In the aforementioned example, once Caitlin hooked Liam in with the dramatic dilemma, Liam was much more inclined to continue the conversation. Remember, the secondary benefit of incorporating interesting angles is that the conversation flows more easily when the other person has more content to connect to and inquire about.

So, what makes an interesting angle? One of the most important factors that determines whether you're engaging and funny or not engaging and not funny is the ability to tap into the emotional side of the human brain instead of its analytical side.

Every fall at my company, there's lots of chatter around various football games, such as Michigan vs. Ohio State, MSU vs Michigan, and so on. I've experimented with different comments over the years, and without fail, the comments dripping with emotion outperform the more analytical comments. Let me give you an example. Next time there's a "big game" coming up, if you say, "I'm feeling pretty nervous about State's chances this time! I'm not sure Smith can pull it off," you'll always get a better, more playful, reaction than if you said, "Smith will need to throw for at least 350 yards if he's going to have a chance to beat Michigan." Both comments share similar sentiments, but underneath they are much different. The first comment stresses emotion, while the second comment taps into the analytical (e.g. talking about scores, points, or player statistics). If your comments are too analytical, you'll trigger your listener to go into analytical mode too—which in many cases is perfectly fine—just don't expect a playful conversation.

Good journalists are exceptional at transforming dry information into interesting stories. They've mastered the art of engagement and know what gets your attention. There's a good reason that news websites don't simply list a bunch of scores under the sports section—readers want an interesting narrative about a player or drama occurring within the sports organization.

Put on your journalist hat and start thinking of ways to refashion your own factual information into more interesting comments. You don't need the creativity of an actual journalist to spin your information into something more interesting.

But what about making people laugh, you ask? Talk to any comedian and they'll tell you that the skill of making people laugh starts by *creating opportunities for laughter*. Like how hypothetical statements often require a strong observation precursor, many fun comments need to be "set up" before the situation is ripe for comedy. People need to be engaged first, then the humor can happen. People need to be in a playful mood. If your angle triggers too many analytical thoughts, you'll make it harder for others to jump into a playful mindset.

The last time I was at the airport, I was slowly making my way through the winding, roped-lined turns of the security checkpoint. As I'm minding my own business, an old man turns to me with a smile, "I was raised on a farm, and this reminds me of when we needed to herd cattle to get milked." What would you say to that old man? A normal response could have been, "Oh yeah? Did you grow up on a farm around here?" Which would have immediately sent the conversation into *information sharing* mode. (Which is completely fine, but not conducive to play.) Instead, my playful nature kicked in and said, "Hopefully *we'll* have better outcomes than those cows!" Why did that work? Not only did it hint at a possible hypothetical outcome, but it made an emotional connection. Seeking information is fine for small talk, but more emotional and hypothetical comments are better for "play talk."

Structure your comments so they're more likely to be interesting to someone and the potential for laughter will increase. There are hundreds of angles—some work better than others. Exaggerating your angles with superlatives helps add interest too. Maybe you're the worst at _____? Or the event you recently attended had the best _____ ever. Open your mind to experimenting with different angles to see what more effectively hooks your audience.

Many angles are compelling because a contrast exists between the statements; a contrast of expectations, observations, actions, etc. For example:

> I was hoping for <u>one thing</u>, but I ended up with <u>something else</u>. I was so bummed.

> I thought it was going to be <u>good/bad</u>, but it turned out <u>bad/good.</u> Why does that always happen to me?

> I didn't like <u>XYZ</u>, but now I do. It's so weird.

> I was shocked; he used to be <u>arrogant/mean/stubborn</u>, but now he's incredibly <u>sweet/nice/carefree</u>.

Hey, speaking of contrasts, it's almost time to learn how super awesome they are in the next chapter.

Homework

The 2019 NBA Finals were played recently. The mighty Golden State Warriors took on the upstart Toronto Raptors. The first game was highlighted by an all-time great performance by a mostly unknown player, named Pascal Siakam. The basketball fans at my workplace discussed the event in multiple ways. Which of the following comments contain interesting angles?

1) He had 32 total points. I think they said he was 4-for-4 at the rim, and 5-for-7 from outside. I would expect him to deliver a similar performance at least a few more times in the series.

2) I heard his performance was the best shooting game anyone's ever had against the Warriors in like three years. He was even playing against one of the best defenders in the game. It was just incredible what he did. I think he might be the key to the Raptors winning it all.

3) I love how he didn't even start playing until he was 16. Apparently he was in seminary school in Cameroon because his dad wanted him to become a priest.

Did you guess? The first example was basically a recital of facts, which is nice, but not necessarily exciting.

Technique #18

Look for Contrasts

The best and most humorous stories almost always contain some contrast.

Real-life Example

Jake loves talking about food. Do you notice anything special about the following comments?

> How do you find time to bake all those cookies?

> I have simple tastes. I'm happy with steak and potatoes.

Of course not. But if Jake adds in some contrasts, his comments become more dynamic and interesting. Check it out:

> How do you have time to bake all those cookies? I barely find time to get home and make a TV Dinner!

> I have simple tastes. I'm happy with steak and potatoes. Keep that *foie gras* and sushi crap away from me!

Why It Works

People love contrasts! Humans are genetically programmed to notice anything conflicting or opposing. Contrasting statements inherently create interesting angles and hook people in. Leverage this psychological principle to your advantage when talking. Point out contrasts in your surroundings or construct your own verbal juxtapositions.

Try this little experiment next time you get a chance: Quickly change your "No" response to a "Yes"—or vice versa—and watch the smile form on the other person's face. "Yes... I mean *no!*" Even the simplest contrasts like the previous example can be entertaining. Luckily, you don't need to be a genius to come up with more contrasts—it's just a matter of structuring your statements a certain way like the "Yes... I mean no" example above.

A popular comedic device is called *The Rule of Three.* The first two things create a pattern, and the third thing breaks the pattern. I coach youth sports, and sometimes I'll get the kids lined up to run on the count of three, but I'll say, "1...2...purple!" And all the kids laugh hysterically. Obviously, they expected me to say "three" but when I said something that conflicted with their expectations, it triggered a humor response. It didn't work the second time I tried it because their expectations adjusted and it was no longer a surprise. Of course, adults probably wouldn't laugh at that contrast, but the underlying principle is the same and applies across all types of comments. Watch President Obama execute this technique in front of Congress in the Recommended Viewing section at the end of the book.

Contrasts are fantastic devices for enhancing and coloring your observations. Your statement may start with an innocent observation, "I like this place," but transform into something much more interesting and playful when you add some contrast and expand on it: "...unlike Geoff's Coffee shop. Have you been to that place? It's a zoo in there! I couldn't even hear myself think."

Let's examine some everyday examples *without* and *with* contrasts so you can compare and "contrast" the two:

Without contrast: I used to have a lot of goals.

With contrast: I used to have a lot of goals... *and then I decided to have kids!*

Without contrast: I really loved it!

With contrast: I didn't think it would be any good, but I actually really loved it!

Here's a longer example:

Jack: Nice tattoo.

Jill: Thanks, do you have any?

Jack: No, I don't.

Jill: My friend got a sword on her arm... she thinks she's edgy now.

Jill failed to incorporate a contrast. Let's give her another chance:

Jill: My friend got a sword on her arm... she thinks she's edgy now. *But she's so not edgy—I don't care how many tattoos she gets!*

In the following example, Michelle asks Joyce what it's like being a new mother. Notice how each contrast is formed by *contrasting against the comment before it.*

Joyce: It's been great...

Joyce's 1st contrast: ...but it's exhausting. I feel like I'm part zombie right now.

Joyce's 2nd contrast: ...but I wouldn't trade it for anything. In a weird way, it's enjoyable to be woken up by this little creature all night.

Joyce's 3rd contrast: ...but if it was anyone else, I'd strangle them!

If you consider what is normal, then you can look for what isn't normal and simply point out the contrast. Contrast your actions/feelings/experiences against their other extremes. For example, if discussing the topic of wine, you could disclose the following statement and stop:

> Initial comment: I love white wine...

Or, you could continue by contrasting your statement against what you don't like or who you're not like, and so on.

> Added contrast: ...and I'm not one of those people who has to drink $70 bottles either—I'll drink anything under ten bucks!

Here's another contrast example: Rick was describing a food truck encounter.

> Rick: I had some great tacos from a food truck down the street.

Like usual, Rick forgot to add any contrast. Let's see what kind of contrast he can add:

> Rick: And it wasn't even a fancy one, it was one of those 'I've been here for 20 years and I've got weeds growing in my engine' food trucks.

Nearly anything can be contrasted. Someone's current behavior with their past behavior. Past thoughts lined up against present thoughts. Let's look at a variety of contrast examples involving self-disclosure statements and observations.

> Initial comment: You went easy on me in there.
>
> Added contrast: ...I thought you were going to crucify me about being late!

> Initial comment: I started working out of my house.

Added contrast: ...until I realized that working out of your house will make you go crazy and start talking to the dog all the time!

Initial comment: Dog boarding places freak me out. Even the ones with open play areas. I feel weird about those places.

Added contrast: ...but I'm probably just being overly paranoid. My dog would probably be like, 'I'd rather go there than hang out with you all day!'

Homework

Now it's your turn. Try to finish the following contrasts (aloud). This practice will start training your brain to structure more statements as interesting and fun contrasts. Remember, these statements could talk about someone or something else rather than yourself. Feel free to alter them as you work your way through.

I hope they _____, because last time they _____.

I was/wasn't expecting _____, but _____ occurred.

I wasn't sure about _____, but I think I'm going to _____.

I didn't think I would like _____, but it turned out to be _____.

It used to be good, but now it's total _____!

I normally do _____, and never noticed _____ until today.

I was supposed to _____, but then _____ changed.

This is good/bad, so much better/worse than _____.

Technique #19

Look for Disagreements and Exceptions

Tap into the power of contrasts and become comfortable with playfully disagreeing and offering exceptions.

Real-life Example

I always get a smile out of people when they ask me what I like to eat because I start with a definitive, "Oh, I'll eat anything, I'm not picky at all..." But then I follow up with an exception, "...except mushrooms. I don't go near fungus!"

Why It Works

Adding an exception after a strong initial statement is a simple technique for creating contrasts. A stronger initial comment often results in better contrast. If I merely stated, "Oh, I usually like seafood or salads... except mushrooms," it doesn't offer the same level of contrast as the original version. Our brains are hard-wired to notice stark contrasts or conflicts.

In the following example, Karen asks Erin how the amusement park was last weekend.

> Erin: It was really fun. Yeah, we enjoyed it a lot.

Just okay, right? Now notice what happens when Erin adds an exception:

> Erin: *...although I spilled soda all over my pants*, but other than that, it was a blast.

Let's examine a few more examples. Exceptions are great for bringing attention to one interesting detail.

Jon: I love you man—*even if you smell like vinegar.*

Jen: You had their green tea? Did you like it?

Brian: I did, I mean, *it looked like sewage water*, but it still tasted good!

Exceptions also help setup hypothetical comments. Jack and Jill talk about making beer.

Jack: I've always wanted to have a home brewery in my basement. That would so cool! *Except I'd probably end up throwing most of it out!*

Jill: Maybe you should have a bakery instead. I think you would like making sweets even more than beer. *Except you would probably end up eating everything before you had a chance to sell it!*

You can get more mileage out of labels and analogies if you qualify and adjust with exceptions afterward. Check out these sexy examples:

He's sexy. He reminds me of my ex... *except with better abs.*

He's sexy. He reminds me of my ex... *except without the beer belly.*

He's sexy. He reminds of the guys on the cover of romance novels... *except without the ripped muscles.*

Clarify or quantify a previous statement; what something *is* or *isn't*, what something *could* or *couldn't do*, and so on.

I feel like I stayed up partying all night—*except I didn't party at all.* I was just being tortured by my four-month-old son, who woke up every hour!

I love people watching—*not in a creepy psycho way though.*

The Playful Disagreement

A disagreement, at its core, is a contrast of opinions. Unfortunately, confrontations, arguments, and disagreements can be a source of angst and discomfort for some people. Obviously, it's important to find commonalities and shared interests, but it's equally important to maintain your individuality. If your sole mission is to please and agree with the other person, you'll end up sounding like a parrot instead of a person. Someone smart once said, "The surest way to failure is to try to please everyone." Besides, lighthearted disagreements add fun and engaging contrasts within a conversation. Check out these:

> Jay: What are you doing?
>
> Joyce: I'm doing my yoga. This is called 'downward-facing dog.'
>
> Jay: It looks more like the 'distressed dog' to me!
>
> Joyce: What's your pose called? *Reclining Sloth?*
>
> Jay: Very funny. No it's actually called *Waiting for Cake.*
>
> Joyce: Do you know the more advanced *Waiting for Cake and Coffee?*
>
> Jay: As a matter of fact, I was hoping you could teach me that one.
>
> Joyce: As soon as I'm finished with my yoga...

> Jeff: That sounds like my friend Rick—he always wears socks with sandals! He's such a dork.
>
> Jill: *Yeah, but he's a lovable dork.*

Technique #20
Play with the Premise
Create contrasts with the underlying premises of a given situation or comment.

Real-life Example

> I divorced my first wife because she was so immature. I'd be in the tub taking a bath and she would walk in whenever she felt like it and sink my boats.

> *-Woody Allen*

Why It Works

So how do Woody Allen jokes translate to funny conversations? You might even call the example a canned joke—which I typically loathe. It's the underlying structure that I want to focus on here.

When you were reading the Woody Allen quote, you probably expected the object of the story (his wife) to be immature. What you didn't expect was for the storyteller himself (Woody) to be the immature one!

Humor often relies on a bit of misdirection. Whenever there is an understood *assumption*, *premise*, or *expectation*, there is an opportunity for a humorous contrast of that assumption, premise, or expectation.

The Woody Allen joke relied on what humorists call "The Reversal" or "The Fake Out," but you can call it "The Ham and Swiss Sandwich" for all I care. Regardless of its name, this type of humor mechanism leads listeners in one direction and then unexpectedly changes direction at the end. Essentially, make them believe you mean one thing when you actually mean the opposite.

As a general rule of thumb, it's better to save the punchline of any type of joke or funny comment for the end. You want to allow for enough build-up of anticipation to occur. For example, my grandpa always said, "The best tool in my garage is my wallet." I get a laugh every time with that line because everyone expects me to mention some kind of tool. Now if the line was, "My wallet is the best tool in my garage," then it loses some of the humor payoff.

Remember, if you have to over-explain your joke, the humor will vanish. Sometimes it's better to keep 'em guessing a little. Start looking for ways you can create contrasts with the expectation or the premise (subtext) of the situation. Think about what is understood, or assumed, and smash that against the proverbial wall.

If I started saying the statement, "He's as sharp as a..." You would have an expectation of what I was going to say next. So, if I finished by saying "...balloon," there would be a moment of surprise. That moment of surprise is where humor often lives.

The more literal, serious, and predictable you are; the more likely you're not saying anything funny. But if you act and say completely unpredictable things, like "He's as sharp as a purple dinosaur," you probably won't create humor either (You may be taken to the nearest psychiatric ward instead!).

Applying the Technique to Conversations

Playing with the premise of a comment or situation typically involves three parts. Let's take a look under the hood:

1. Consider the underlying premise/subtext of the situation.
2. Consider what someone probably expects to happen next.

3. Instead of saying/doing what is expected, move along the *premise continuum* toward its opposite end. Which helps you reverse or flip the premise.

Premise continuums? What?? Stay with me for a minute. Let's break down a more involved interaction to see how to play with a premise in conversation.

Jake and his date, Lorraine, slow dance together at a wedding.

Lorraine: Oh, I love your cologne...

What is the basic premise of her statement? What is understood here? That *Jake put on cologne,* right? Jake clearly put on cologne because Lorraine can smell it. Jake would be expected to say something predictable like, "Thank you, it's Hugo Boss." Lorraine would most likely follow up with something standard like, "Oh that's nice."

Nothing funny, right? What would happen if Jake mentally traveled down the *premise continuum* to its opposite end? The "Anti-premise" if you will. The opposite of the premise ("Jake put on cologne") is that Jake *didn't put on cologne,* so the scent must be *from something else.* With me so far? What else could the scent be from? Did Jake spill a strawberry margarita on himself earlier? That would be a funny reason. This explanation works too:

Jake: Thank you, but actually, it's my *natural scent,* do you like it?

The aforementioned response is a direct confrontation and contrast of Lorraine's expectations and usually earns a laugh or at least a smile. Jake might respond by talking about how *he's an alien and that's how alien's smell;* but that would be too far off the spectrum and probably not funny. The comment should still be relevant to the premise and in the realm of possibility. It's possible that Jake's natural scent smells nice, right? It's possible that he spilled a strawberry margarita on himself, also. Either would work great.

Anyway, what happens next is the magic of humor and playfulness. Once Jake jumps into the play zone, Lorraine joins him.

> Lorraine: Really? You should bottle that scent—you could make a fortune.
>
> Jake: You think? Would you help me bottle it? I'll need a *good distributor.*
>
> Lorraine: Definitely... and it needs a good name, like Mountain Air, by Jake.
>
> Jake: Great idea! Or maybe...

Starting to make sense yet? Good, let's look at some more examples. I was working at my cubicle one day when a coworker, Patrick, came over and asked a question about my strange shark-fin looking computer mouse.

> Patrick: What kind of mouse is that?
>
> Me: It's ergonomic; it prevents you from getting carpal tunnel when you're older. You should try it.

What's the expected response here? That my friend would say something like, "Oh, that's cool. I could use one of those." Or, "That's nice, but I don't have any wrist issues." However, instead of the expected comments, my friend offered a perfect anti-premise that made me laugh.

> Patrick: Cool, but what if I *want* carpal tunnel when I'm older? I mean, it's always been a goal of mine to develop sore wrists.

Playing with the premise takes on many forms; sometimes it's simple and quick like the following:

Lyndsey: I think his career is over.

Chad: I don't think it ever started!

Chad understood the premise and then responded with a comment based on the other end of the premise spectrum.

I was listening to a coworker share some news with another coworker:

Brent: Did you see that the cafeteria has healthier, organic ketchup now?

Colleen: I did. I didn't think I'd like it, but it's pretty good.

Brent: It probably doesn't have all that high fructose corn syrup anymore.

Colleen: Yeah, now it just has *organic* high fructose corn syrup!

Colleen perfectly played with the premise of Brent's claim: The ketchup contains only healthy ingredients. Similarly, she could have flipped to the other end of the premise spectrum with a remark like, "Yeah, now it only contains 9 grams of sugar instead of 10!" Both cases act like it's *barely* healthier, if at all.

Irony is another popular form of playing with the premise. Make more fun statements that contradict something that has just been said. For example, someone just finished telling you that you're a good listener. You could then respond, "What was that?"

Next time you're watching a TV comedy, look out for funny premise contradictions. For example, a character, let's call him Bob, could be talking about how healthy he is, and then immediately proceed to eat a large deep-dish pizza. That would be an example of someone's actions contrasting against the understood premise of his spoken words.

Homework

Let's try a playing with the premise exercise. You and your friends are talking about posting fairly personal info on Facebook.

> Kenny: Be careful, Zuckerberg's going to sell all your private info to the Russians.

What's the premise or subtext here? His statement only works because it *assumes* you care about your information being sold to Russians. You could say, "Yeah, you're right. I should be more careful." But that's not funny. What if you pretend like you *don't care* about your info being stolen?

There are other premises to play with here, too. Another premise underlying his statement is that your information is worth something of value to the Russians. What if it wasn't worth anything?

Another possible premise: Kenny assumes that you're not Russian. So, it could be humorous if you *are* actually a Russian citizen. Or, better yet, what about a Russian spy? What if you're actually Putin's grandson?

Can you think of a funny response to Kenny's comment? Here are a few ideas to spark your imagination:

> That's fine, my info is probably worth about 3 cents and a bag of Skittles.
>
> If the Russians paid for my info, they'd want a refund!
>
> Maybe I actually work for the Russians.
>
> Well, I'd get more friend requests then, right?

Technique #21

Make It Trivially Significant

An effortless way to create playful, humorous, and unexpected contrasts is by simply overreacting or underreacting.

Real-life Example

> Caitlyn: What was it that attracted you to me when we first met?
>
> Liam: I loved your infectious smile and your willingness to help everyone around you.

Was that funny? No, of course not. Caitlyn expected a serious/significant response, and Liam delivered. If Liam wanted to play with the premise (see the previous technique), he could have gone to the extreme other end of the premise with something playful like the following:

> Liam: Honestly, I loved that you had five fingers on each hand. That was a huge turn on!
>
> Caitlyn: Oh, you shouldn't flatter me so much!
>
> Liam: I was getting sick of all those four-fingered women I kept dating. You showed up in my life and I was thrilled!

Why It Works

Treating a trivial situation as something more significant, or a weighty situation as something trivial, is an easy-to-cook recipe for humor. In either case, the premise is being played with to create a contrast. In Liam's case, he knew Caitlyn was introducing a significant and heavy topic, so he talked about something very light as the reason for falling for her. He could have said he fell for her feet, the fact that she liked Cheerios, or some other trivial observation, and all notes of levity would have worked equally as well. (This style is often referred to as "irreverent humor.")

Let's take a look at another example of levity in conversation:

> Steph: I'm looking forward to this birthday party. Did you get him a present yet?

Serious topic introduced. Kenny should have bought a present. And maybe Kenny did buy a present, but nonetheless, he decides to execute this technique anyway for the fun of it.

> Kenny: Yeah, I did. I have a few Jolly Ranchers in my pocket. I'll save some cherry ones for him.

> Steph: Yeah, that will go over well! He'll be like, 'Gee, thanks—*I always wanted a cherry Jolly Rancher for my birthday!*'

> Kenny: And since it's probably covered in lint, we won't even need to wrap it! I call that a *win-win*.

Following a serious comment with a lighthearted response can lead to a laugh or a smack to the face if the other person isn't in a playful mood, so watch yourself!

The safer bet is to counter trivial topics with serious responses (a la the YouTube Reaction video creators from Technique #7). When you come across something fairly frivolous, act like it's much more significant or dramatic than it really is. Overreact to small and unimportant things in your environment. You can also place artificial significance on your own trivial actions or personal experiences. There is tremendous opportunity for humor with this technique because most life experiences, like eating breakfast, driving to work, taking out the garbage, etc., generally aren't very important or consequential.

Check out the following example of someone overreacting to something trivial. Richard and Betty are on their second date:

Betty: I actually don't really like hot fudge sundaes—I never have.

Richard: What? You don't like hot fudge sundaes? I don't know if this is going to work out then. I can only date people who like hot fudge sundaes.

Betty: But I like caramel sundaes, doesn't that count?

Richard: I might make an exception for caramel sundaes, but I'm going to have to ask my friends what they think about this situation.

Technique #22

Observational Humor

Look for insignificant everyday things that could take on a larger role.

Real-life Example

Rowan is known for always dressing professionally, but one day he showed up to work looking more disheveled than normal.

> Maureen: Wow, your shirt is actually *un-tucked*! Are you okay?
>
> Rowan: I know. It's because I'm going to the cider mill later. I feel so weird. Please don't think any less of me.
>
> Maureen: I'm just not sure how I feel about that. I mean, it's going to take me a while to get used to it.
>
> Rowan: This is one of the rare days, every year, when it happens. So, enjoy it now, while it lasts. Tomorrow the shirt will be tucked, and you'll have only memories of this day.

Why It Works

I should have just titled this chapter "Jerry Seinfeld." He was—and always will be—the master of finding humor in the insignificant and trivialities of life. (Watch re-runs of his old show if you haven't yet.) He zooms in on the mundane, finds the commonality we all experience, and finds the absurd aspects of it. Remember, if you find something strange or nonsensical, it's likely others will too if you describe it accurately. Share more of the quirky subtleties of your life experiences and observations of everyday things.

This type of humor works remarkably well for conversation and is also extremely low-risk and fun. Observational humor borrows from the concepts we covered earlier about playing with the premise and treating something trivial as more significant than it really is. This was also introduced in Technique #7, React Like a YouTuber.

As I sit here writing this, one coffee barista just told the other, "I'm so impressed by your ability to slice that cheesecake in half... *you have the hands of a brain surgeon*." Slicing cheesecake isn't a big deal but being so impressed with something so trivial can be fun. Her comment made everyone chuckle, including the customers listening.

Here's a little-known fact about me: I have a tendency to add water to my coffee as a way to slow down my caffeine intake throughout the day. When a colleague observed me adding water into my freshly poured cup of premium roast coffee, he stood there like he saw a ghost, and exclaimed, "*Did you really just pour water in your coffee? What are you—some kind of barbarian? Were you raised by wolves? What are you going to do next—add orange juice?*" My colleague observed a unique event and capitalized on it for some quick humor. Of course, I realize how gross it looks to some people and we both had a good laugh over it.

In the following example from *Seinfeld*, Cosmo Kramer overreacts to the way Jerry talks about dentists:

> Jerry: So, you won't believe what happened with Whatley today. It got back to him that I made this little dentist joke, and he got all offended! Those people can be so touchy.
>
> Kramer: 'Those people'? Listen to yourself!

Jerry: What?

Kramer: You think that dentists are so different from me and you? They came to this country just like everybody else in search of a dream!

Jerry: Whatley's from Jersey!

Kramer: And now he's a full-fledged American!

Jerry: Kramer, he's just a dentist.

Kramer: And you're an anti-dentite!

Jerry: I am *not* an anti-dentite!

Kramer: You're a rabid anti-dentite! Oh, it starts with a few jokes and some slurs: 'Hey, denty!' Next thing you know you'll be saying, 'They should have their own schools'!

Jerry: They *do* have their own schools!

"The Yada Yada." *Seinfeld: Episode 152.* Ethan Brown, 1997.

The basic formula here is fairly simple:

1. Look for an insignificant thing that could take on a larger role.
2. Exaggerate its characteristics, its goals, its possible impact, its significance, and so on. Question why it exists, why it is the way it is, where it's going, or where it came from.
3. Provide supporting examples to prove your point if applicable.

Jerry Seinfeld was famous for starting his jokes with, "What's the deal with..." For example, if you have a strand of hair that will stubbornly not go down, you could just ignore it. But instead, remember WWJD (What Would Jerry Do); point it out, exaggerate its features, talk about how it's affecting you, give it a name, and/or give it intentions. Talk about how it's an "overachiever" or how it's trying to rebel against the rest of the hair.

It's amazing how much potential comedic content is out there if you're looking for it. Ever heard of the phrase "Don't sweat the small stuff"? A lot of humor relies on *pretending* to sweat the small stuff.

For example, your laptop feels hot on your lap. Exaggerate it: "This laptop is burning me. I think the top of my pants are melting. I can smell the slight burning of my thigh skin." Question it: "Who created this thing? Did they forget the cooling fan? Were cooling fans not available while they built my laptop? Why did you buy this for me? Were you trying to scar me?" Of course it's not necessary to ask all those questions, but I think you get the idea.

You're watching TV and you notice multiple drug commercials have aired in a row. How could you exaggerate your observation? Here's one way: "All the commercials are trying to sell drugs now. I don't see anything else. Is this what our economy has come to? Are we either selling or buying drugs? Is that our entire economy? What has this country become?"

Here's a slightly more robust version stemming from the same observation above: "All the commercials are trying to sell drugs now. And the people always look so happy. How are they always so happy? I want to buy them all just so I can look that happy. And they lure you in by saying things like, 'Do you ever feel *hungry*? Then maybe you need Viavomeyra.' Why yes, sometimes I do feel hungry, I'll take some Viavomeyra. I don't know—now I'm questioning myself. Do I really need it? And who comes up with those names? Do they walk into 4th grade classrooms and ask all the kids to come up with the silliest names possible?"

As tempting as it is to share your observations of the world around you and the people you interact with, it's also important to observe yourself. Self-observations are the safest kind because it's difficult to offend anyone if you're targeting yourself, which leaves the door wide open for extreme exaggerations and embellishments. And I get it, many of you reading this are hesitant to talk about yourselves and may despise narcissists who ramble incessantly about themselves. But I'm here to tell you that being a little narcissistic is necessary for a lot of comedic techniques. Do it for the sake of laughter. Talk about yourself and your silly quirks more. Share more funny stories about your life. For example:

> I'm always late to _____. I end up pissing everyone off because I _____.
>
> I never eat _____. It grosses me out that they _____.
>
> I'm kind of obsessed with _____. Don't tell anyone, if anyone found out, I'd _____.

One summer, I was staying at a cabin with some friends and overheard an entertaining argument about something very trivial. It began with Mike disclosing an inconsequential detail about his bedtime routine.

> Mike: I wash my face *before* I brush my teeth.
>
> Michele: I actually do the opposite.
>
> Mike: Well, that's the *wrong order*. Everyone knows it's teeth after face. Something to do with the pores being sensitive.
>
> Michele: I've never done it that way in my entire life.
>
> Mike: Well that makes sense now. Because so many things you do are backwards. This answer a lot of questions.

> Michele: Who decided the correct order anyway? Did you
> learn that from a class you took in high school?

When both participants are in a playful mood, arguments about trivial topics like the correct order of bedtime hygiene routines can be a lot of fun.

Homework

Pay more attention to what you find interesting (or annoying) in the world. Look for patterns or strange coincidences. Analyze those moments where you stop and say, "Huh. That's interesting." Expand on it. Why is it interesting? What else could be funny about it if you exaggerated some aspect of it? I find mint chocolate ice cream interesting because chocolate and mint are typically two flavors not associated with each other. When you brush your teeth with toothpaste, the last thing you think is, "Hey, I'd love to mix this toothpaste flavor with chocolate." What other flavors would sound strange mixed with chocolate? What other strange combinations exist in the world?

Technique #23

Sneak in Some Sarcasm

Make funnier comments with understatements or overstatements.

Real-life Examples

You visit your friend's house. They have a toddler, Ethan, and you notice blue and red crayon marks all over their living room wall. You could state the obvious: "Looks like Ethan drew all over your wall," but that's boring. Let's try some good old' fashioned sarcasm—for example:

> Hey, I like the new wall decorations... they're very bohemian.
>
> Nice wall décor... what style is that? French modern?
>
> Does Home Depot sell those paint colors?

Why It Works

I know, you're probably aware of the concept of sarcasm. However, it's important to look under the hood in order to improve your ability to wield such an important comedic device.

Sarcasm is usually as simple as stating something that contradicts the apparent truth. One of the most common sarcastic statements said thousands of times a day across the country is when the weather is terrible: "Beautiful day we're having, huh?"

The contradictions can be as colorful and exaggerated as you want. Remarking, "I like the new wall decorations," when it's obvious that a child accidentally colored on the wall is good wholesome sarcasm. Exaggerating, or questioning its existence with comments like, "It's very bohemian," or "Does Home Depot sell those colors?" continues the playful observation and takes it to the next level. (See previous technique in case you skipped it.) Similarly, Ethan's mom could have playfully responded to your initial sarcasm, "Oh yeah, I know a good interior decorator if you want a similar design for your house."

I was at the movies and watching the previews. After a preview for a particularly depressing movie, the guy next to me said to his date, "Well, that sure looks like a lighthearted comedy." His date erupted in laughter and found his comment hilarious. I'm not sure it was *that* hilarious, but it was still more entertaining than stating the obvious!

When presented with any situation, you typically have three choices for offering your observation/opinion:

1. *Overstate* and exaggerate the facts of the situation.

2. *State* the facts exactly as they are.

3. *Understate* and downplay or deny the facts of the situation.

Which option would you say boring people prefer? You guessed it, boring people like Literal Larry prefer the second option and tend to state observations as literally and factually as possible. However, if you need to say something obvious, it can be twice as interesting and entertaining if you simply understate or overstate it. People often enjoy a little intrigue or layer of sarcasm; make 'em guess a little. Let's look at a few examples of these indirect statements.

You visit your friend Abbie, and her dog Ben jumps on you and smothers you with giant slobbery kisses.

Literal Observation: Your dog really likes me.

Understatement: I have a feeling your dog likes me.

Understatement 2: Do you think your dog likes me?

Understatement 3: I don't think your dog likes me very much.

Overstatement: I think your dog wants to marry me!

Let's try another dog example, because why not? Dogs are awesome. You're at Margaret's house this time. She has a cute little Pug Boxer mix named Tucker, who barks at you when you arrive. Margaret could make a number of comments:

Literal Observation: He won't scare many people away.

Understatement: I don't think he would even scare away the mice!

Overstatement: No one would ever break into my house with such an intimidating beast guarding the place.

Sarcasm, in my not-so-humble opinion, gives you the best bang for the buck if you're looking for easy but effective comedic conversation techniques. It's not too hard to get right, it's not too risky, and it sometimes makes people smile or laugh. You'll rarely get the reaction that a well-placed hypothetical statement can garner, but sarcasm is much easier to slip into everyday conversation.

One time I was giving a new co-worker a tour and introducing them to everyone. I stopped by Mike's desk and said, "This is Mike, he handles the knowledge database. He's very helpful if you need anything." And Mike could have just agreed, but instead, he lightened up the exchange by sarcastically denying everything I just said, "Actually, I'm not helpful at all. I'm actually very selfish and like to keep to myself." We all laughed. There was nothing inherently witty about his comments, but they directly and unexpectedly contradicted the truth I just laid out. Here are some more examples:

You see an old half-eaten sandwich on the street.

That looks delicious!

You receive a letter in the mail. You notice that your name is completely butchered.

I'm sure this must be important!

You see a guy with hair spiked about a foot high.

I'm not sure his hair is high enough... maybe we should see if he needs more hair gel so he can get it a few inches taller.

Keep in mind, at the heart of sarcasm are some elements of playing with the premise (Technique #20). When you and your friends see a gross half-eaten sandwich on the ground, you're expected to comment about how gross and nasty it is, because that's what's generally understood, right? If you travel down the opposite end of the premise spectrum, a great alternative is to talk about how you'd actually like to eat it for lunch. In the aforementioned example, where I introduced Mike, his response perfectly played with the premise, creating a fun contrast.

I was listening to one of my favorite podcasts, *Conan O'Brien Needs a Friend*, and in one particular episode he opened up with, "Because it's time a middle-aged-white man had a podcast in America." Conan understands an underlying premise very well: that there's an overabundance of people in his demographic doing podcasts (and late night TV shows for that matter). So he decided to sarcastically make light of the underlying premise by acting like America needed him to be the face of such an "underrepresented" demographic.

Homework

Joyce and Jason are house shopping. They tour a lovely home but suddenly notice it has a tiny backyard.

>Joyce: I don't know about this house. Look at how small the backyard is. We couldn't do much gardening back there.

Joyce sticks to the facts. How could Jason lighten up the mood with some sarcasm? Think of how he could understate or overstate the problem. What could be grown back there? What could or couldn't fit? Try to think of a few comments before reading any further!

>Yeah, we could. We could probably grow two, maybe three carrots. But they'd have to be baby carrots.

>Wow, it's tiny. But I could probably mow the lawn with a pair of scissors, so that's nice.

>Just think, we could grow enough food to feed a family of squirrels for like a week.

>That's the biggest yard I've ever seen. I'm so shocked the realtor didn't mention it as one of the benefits. We should build a pool with a waterfall and put it right over there.

Did you notice how nicely the hypotheticals and sarcasm play together? Let's dive into adding more hypotheticals next.

Technique #24

Add Hypotheticals to Your Opinions

Hypotheticals not only help you paint more colorful descriptions; they add a new playful dimension to your opinions.

Real-life Examples

Check out these normal, everyday observations and opinions:

> I love reading. A lot.
>
> It cost $50,000? That's expensive.
>
> That's risky. I'm not doing that.
>
> It has 50 grams of sugar? That's a lot.
>
> That's impossible. You won't find it.
>
> That looks gross. I wouldn't drink it.
>
> You do an amazing goat impersonation.

Now let's rephrase each one by adding a colorful hypothetical comment (*italicized*) to support each initial comment.

> I love reading. *I'd live in the basement of a bookstore if they'd let me.*
>
> It cost $50,000? That's expensive. *That's a down payment on a house!*
>
> That's risky. I'm not doing that. *You'd have to buy me lunch at Panera every single day for three months straight.*
>
> It has 50 grams of sugar? *You might as well be drinking a glass of corn syrup!*
>
> That's impossible. *You'd be better off trying to find Atlantis.*
>
> That looks gross. *If I just arrived from being stranded in the Sahara Desert, I still wouldn't drink that crap.*

You do an amazing goat impersonation. *You'll be playing in Vegas in two years.*

Why It Works

Hypothetical statements help improve other techniques, like playing with the premise and sarcasm. The more techniques you practice, the more you can combine them for even funnier interactions. Let's look at some examples:

During the last election cycle, I was driving around town and noticed a street corner had more than five signs for the same candidate: Richard Henterly. Big, small, different colors, and yep, all for the same guy. What's the obvious premise there? It's a gratuitous amount of signage—completely unnecessary.

What would the literal observation sound like? Literal Larry may point out, "That's a lot of signs." But the funny person would play with the premise and say, "I don't know if Richard has enough signs." Adding a sarcastic hypothetical could make the observation even better. "He may want to talk to his sign guy and see about adding a few more. Maybe tape some small ones on top of big ones and make like a sign pyramid, just in case people don't notice the other 12 signs next to it." This also taps into the secret of Seinfeld's success—exaggerate the absurdities of everyday life. If you look for absurdities, you'll find 'em. (Except for in my book. Nothing absurd here. Keep moving along.)

At a kid's birthday party, the father, Dan, decides it would be a good idea to hold up the piñata with his hand. The four-year-olds proceed to line up to hit the piñata with a bat. One obvious premise in this situation: *Dan risks being hit with a bat and possibly hurt.*

If the premise is understood by the people in attendance, it's not always necessary to make an overt observation: "The kids are going to hit Dan with a bat." Instead, utilize the premise and state some sarcastic observations with a little hypothetical flare mixed in. Check out these possibilities:

Dan, *I hope you have good health insurance!*

I hope you have some padding under those pants!

You don't really need your left hand anyway!

They work because they leverage an understood premise and also tap into the imaginations of the people watching.

In the following example, notice how Rick delivers a strong opinion, and then follows it up with various hypothetical possibilities:

Rick: What are you up to tonight?

Frank: My girlfriend invited some people over from church to have a book club discussion tonight.

Rick: *That sounds terrible.* I don't think I could think of a worse Friday night than hanging out with random church strangers.

Frank: Yeah, tell me about it

Rick: With the exception of being hauled away in a state cruiser, or being mauled by a stray dog, I don't think it gets worse than that.

Frank: And apparently they might need to use my grill to cook dinner.

Rick: Wait a minute. You're saying that some stranger's going to use your grill at your own house? That violates all kinds of man codes. No other man should be touching another man's grill. Next thing you know, you're gonna come home to find grease stains all over your new microsuede recliner.

Rick beautifully setup many hypothetical possibilities and delivered some fun examples. What else could Frank have come home to? A broken Xbox? Someone driving his car? Someone adding more chlorine to his pool? Someone making out with his girlfriend behind the tool shed? There are all kinds of scenarios if stretch your imagination.

Look for Patterns

Look for patterns you can exaggerate and push to the edges of reality. A few of us were talking about taking a vacation, and my friend Bill said, "My aunt's got a house in South Carolina, maybe we could stay there." Shortly after, he also mentioned that one of his Uncle's had a house in Florida we might be able to stay at also. So now there's a *pattern*: Bill has family in a few good vacation spots. Your observation could push the noticeable pattern to the max. "Apparently, Bill has family in every possible vacation spot in the world," which then sets up additional hypothetical commentary like, "Do you have any Chinese cousins, so we could visit Hong Kong?"

I was listening to *Conan O'Brien Needs a Friend* (with Tim Olyphant, 2019), and Conan's friend and guest on the show, Tim, wasn't paying attention at all to anything Conan was saying. Conan called out his friend's pattern of behavior with a beautiful and hilarious hypothetical metaphor:

Corralling you is, wow, very difficult. You're like a kitten at a rave, you're just all over the map. You're distracted by

colors... you're spinning... you're pawing at the air. People
are picking you up, you get loose, and you run around again.
I am trying to get a cogent interview and it's impossible.

Tim astutely replied, "Always lands on his feet though." During
the same conversation, Conan observed another pattern about
how relaxed and cool Tim always appears, and then added to it
with some extra playful hypothetical details:

You're always so laid back and chill. You're a guy who shows
up, and you've got your Panama hat and your boardshorts.
And you're wearing your saratchos... clubatos... I'm making
up words now.

Sometimes Conan will contrast the established pattern against
his own personal behavior or description, as he did after stating
the aforementioned observation:

...When I wear shorts, people call an ambulance. They think,
'What's wrong with him?'

Playing right along, Tim remarked about Conan's notorious
paleness, "You reflect a lot of light, so at first it's, 'What's that
bright object coming this way?' So that throws them."

And because this has become the Tim and Conan section of my
book, let's include one more Tim and Conan example. Tim and
Conan were talking about what occurs when they venture out in
public together. Conan was frustrated with how people act around
him, "I always get people who yell, 'DO IT!' I don't even know what
that means. I could be at a restaurant, and the server might be like,
'You might want to try the celery soup,' and out of nowhere
someone shouts, 'DO IT!'" Notice how Conan started with a pattern,
and then supported it with a hypothetical example? Now you know

all of Conan's secrets—if you go out and become a rich and famous talk show host, don't forget about me!

Look for life's patterns (and funny coincidences) and call them out, because after you establish a pattern, you can add a hypothetical to support it.

The popular social platform, Reddit, is always good for laughs. There have been a bunch of political posts lately that introduce a pattern and are followed up by hypothetical examples. For instance, in a recent poll, all 20+ Democratic candidates for President were beating Trump in a head-to-head match-up. What's the pattern there? Essentially, anyone who has decided to run is beating him. So how could you push that pattern into more extreme territory? Who else could beat him? Justin Bieber? Kenny G? For example, "I heard Big Bird is polling at 45%, Trump, 39%."

Check out some other popular phrase structures for calling out patterns:

> You always _____ when I walk/say/eat/do _____. Does that mean I'm _____?

> How come everything Keanu does is _____? If we were all _____, he'd still do _____!

> Have you ever noticed that every time I come home, he _____? If I moved to another house, would he _____ too?

Many of your supporting hypotheticals might naturally create contrasts against the initial pattern, like the following:

> All the kids know how to _____, except my son, he'd rather just do _____.

> I always _____ before a test/date/drive/run. Maybe just once I should _____?

All the sheep are walking around and eating, except for that
big _____, he's just sitting there, acting like _____.

The Secret Life

Another way to insert hypothetical comments into observations
and sarcasm is by exploring possible hidden agendas and ulterior
motives. Make up some fun secret motivations.

Saying "You're secretly a Marilyn Manson fan, aren't you? I
knew it!" can be fun if their music tastes are much different than
the band you claim they admire.

Remember all the observations about the baby from Technique
7, React Like a YouTuber? Those observations were mostly
pertaining to the baby's appearance. When you think more in
terms of hypotheticals, your observations can go far beyond literal
observations about appearance, like, "He's so handsome."
Speculate as to what the baby hypothetically desires, despises,
dislikes, hopes and dreams!

For example, maybe Jan is taking a lot of photos of the new baby
when he starts becoming cranky. Possible funny observations
could include:

Maybe he just doesn't like that angle. Try the other side.

I think he's worried it'll go viral.

He's just camera shy.

Maybe you should talk to his agent first.

Maybe he thinks you're just paparazzi... I don't blame him.

The sky's the limit for secret intentions. Don't forget about
anthropomorphism (attributing human traits to animals or
objects). Did a squirrel just run in front of your car? Well, he

probably *wanted* you to have an accident. Maybe he was showing his girlfriend how brave he was? Is the printer in your office not working for you? Maybe it's mad at you for printing so many color copies? Maybe it's just not a morning kind of printer. Check out this real interaction:

> Joe: They canceled my favorite show. Turbo Tucker is no longer on.
>
> Libby: They did? That sucks!
>
> Joe: How come it's only my shows that get canceled? I don't know what the Netflix execs have against me.

Joe's comment gave Netflix executives a secret agenda targeting him personally. Feel free to make up secret agendas, goals, habits, or thoughts for friends in a playful way as well. For example, a few friends, Jake, Justin, and Lorraine visit the zoo:

> Loraine: It says here that the lions sleep more than 20 hours a day!
>
> Justin: That sounds like Jake—he'd fit right in here.

Homework

Say the following aloud and fill in the blanks with whatever you want. Don't worry if your idea doesn't make total sense. The point is to condition your mind to leverage more hypothetical phrase structures with your opinions. Practice these comments over and over until you need to take a bathroom break. Then come back and practice some more.

> Why is he just standing there like that? He probably wants to _____.

She's creepy. She looks like she's about to _____ all over the place.

That's horrible! I'd rather do _____ than that.

What is that guy thinking? Does he think we're going to just _____?

He looks scary. What if _____?

I love it there. If I was rich I would _____.

Technique #25

Reveal Your Playful Secrets

You could pretend to be, do, or like all kinds of things in the name of humor.

Real-life Example

Entering work, Andy encounters his co-worker, Bill, who makes a general observation about the recent theft of a floor mat.

> Bill: The floors are so slippery in here now—who on earth would steal a 50-foot-long floor mat?
>
> Andy: I know, that's really strange.

But of course Andy's response is nothing special. He could lighten up the mood by adding something more playful:

> Andy: Okay, I wasn't going to tell you... but I had to borrow it.
>
> Bill: Oh yeah?
>
> Andy: I have a really long, narrow house! It's perfect in my entryway.

Why It Works

Bill clearly knew that Andy wasn't responsible for the theft, so it was funny for Andy to pretend he was involved. The previous chapter covered giving other people or things secret intentions, but what about giving yourself secret intentions and ulterior motives? Injecting yourself as the reason for something seemingly unrelated to you can be an easy way to walk into some humor.

There are a multitude of other ways to offer playful self-disclosure if you look:

- Pretend to be part of the cause or solution to something.
- Pretend to be involved with something that no one would have suspected.
- Pretend to be an example of why something works or doesn't work.
- Pretend to feel or think the opposite of what anyone would suspect.

Let's look at another example. Two friends, Joe and Jason, are discussing a news article about the Russian figure skating team making some changes to their workout regimen.

> Jason: Yeah, it looks like they're trying to make skating more manly.
>
> Joe: That's why they asked me to join their team—I had to turn them down though. They couldn't pay me enough.

It's also easy to pretend to have ulterior motives. Maybe you're at a corporate event and want to start a conversation as you're in line for food. I've heard the following all work successfully:

> I don't know about you, but I'm just here for the free dessert.
>
> These look delicious. Don't tell, but I may have to come back for seconds or even thirds.
>
> I think I might just steal these turkey wraps to bring home for dinner.

Not only is it fun to disclose secret playful motives, but don't leave out secret hobbies, likes, dislikes, experiences, and more.

I was meeting a friend for lunch, and upon arrival, my friend launched into a mini-tirade about how hard it was to find a parking spot because some rude person took up three parking spaces with their truck. Responding, "I hate when people do that" would have been acceptable, but acting like *I was the rude truck driver* has more humor potential. "Sorry, that was actually me, I just don't like anyone to park too close to me. I have a weird car phobia."

When someone shares a unique experience, it's *assumed* that you probably didn't have the same experience. That assumption is the premise, and because it's assumed that you didn't have a similar experience, revealing that you *did* can be a surprising twist. The conflict is often humorous when it's clear that you're playing.

Talk show hosts frequently use the "fake similarity" trick to gain a quick laugh. Often a guest reveals some unique personal tidbit or anecdote. For example: "When I was young, my parents often took me to a llama farm... it was a lot of fun." To which the host acts like they too share the experience in some way. "I know this sounds crazy, but I actually *own* a llama farm."

Look out for something unique or interesting about what the other person said and pretend to share that thing in common. Check a few examples out:

> Anna: My son keeps peeing on the floor during potty training. He's so bad—he just can't control his bladder yet.

> Bryan: It's not his fault—*I can't control mine either*! I must have skipped potty training day.

Zak runs into Mike at the grocery store and reaches out to shake his hand.

> Mike: Hey! Sorry I'm kind of gross and sweaty, I just finished working out!

> Zak: That's okay, *I'm gross and sweaty too*. But I don't have a good excuse!

Sometimes there's an opportunity to embellish and twist the fake similarity into something even funnier, like the following example.

> Joe: My brothers and I wrestled every single day when I was a kid. I think that's why I became such a good athlete later.
>
> Justin: Yeah, we did too. But I usually just wrestled my mom. And she always won. Then I would feel bad and go find my 90-year-old grandma. She was a little easier, but she still kicked my butt. And I never became a good athlete later.

And sometimes it's funny to pretend to have a similar experience or preference, but ultimately disclose something that completely antithetical. Read the following example to understand what I mean: One time my friend, Julie, told me about how she's training for an ultra-marathon race (100 miles), and ran for over two hours before breakfast that morning. She's hoping to shave over an hour from her time from last year. I responded, "Wow, that's impressive. I walked for about two minutes from my car to my desk this morning. And I'm hoping to get my time down to about 1.8 minutes."

What's Your Backstory?

In case you haven't guessed yet, I have a minor comedy crush on Conan O'Brien; I consider him the master of conversational humor. Fortunately, he launched a podcast as I was wrapping up my book so I could truly analyze a ton of his informal (and not just pre-planned talk show material) conversations. The bad news—Conan possesses a memory for pop culture and facts that few could rival.

But we can still learn from his techniques. One thing we can all learn from him his how often he incorporates his own backstory.

I intentionally use the word "backstory" because that's often a term reserved for what writers create for characters. Conan masterfully weaves his own backstory into nearly every conversation at some point. But instead of just self-disclosing interesting information, his factual information serves as the springboard for playful and fabricated hypothetical stories.

Conan O'Brien's podcast co-host, Sona Movsesian, one time mentioned, "I bit my nails as a kid." (Conan O'Brien Needs a Friend, with Hannah Gatsby, 2019) That was all Conan needed to reference something similar he did as a child. "You were a nail biter? When I was a kid, we always sucked our thumbs, so our mom put on this poison nail polish stuff to try to stop us. It worked...until I slept and sucked on my thumb all night." I'm not quoting him exactly in this example, but that's essentially what he said. And that was the factual foundation. Once he connects to the conversation with the factual, relevant details, he tends to launch into more playful territory. In this case, there are many options. For example, he could say, "I must have had some weird sucking fetish. Maybe that explains why I still like to suck on my toes every morning before breakfast. You should keep your fingers away from me. I might be tempted." Or he could go down a different zany path, like: "I got the worst headache from that stuff. And now I have an addiction to harsh chemicals—*thanks mom!* Yeah, I'm still in therapy for it. Don't let me near your hairspray."

A lot of you reading this don't reveal a lot of personal information. But I'm here to remind you that your humor will primarily come from two sources: 1) comments about your surroundings, and 2) comments about yourself. If you don't feel comfortable talking about yourself or your past/future, you're limiting your potential for humor by 50.3%, to be exact. (Don't ask where I came up with that figure.)

Technique #26

Be a Play Partner

There is almost no greater conversational crime than throwing a wet blanket on a newly introduced, playful comment. Be a good conversation partner and play along.

Real-life Example

After months of Arctic-like weather in Michigan, the temperature finally escaped the low teens and hit 45 degrees Fahrenheit. (Obviously not very warm, but much hotter than the low teens!) Jill introduced a little playful sarcasm to the group:

> Jill: Are you enjoying this *heat wave*?
>
> Jack: Oh yeah, I think I might get the pool open!
>
> Justin: Should we bring over some steaks to grill?
>
> Jon: It's not going to be hot enough for all that.

Why It Works

Obviously, Jon was the wet blanket in the previous scenario. Make sure the play doesn't stop with you—that would be a cardinal sin in improv comedy. How could Jon have played along with the sarcastic "heat wave" comment? He could have pretended it was hot and talked about wearing shorts, washing his car, or any number of classic summer activities that follow the heatwave theme introduced by Jill.

Next time someone throws a playful comment your way, instead of dropping the ball or jumping back into the serious zone, *pretend it's true* and think about ways to play along. Sometimes it's about pretending the hypothetical scenario they painted is real.

What would be the impact on you or others? How could you exaggerate the hypothetical even further?

A friend shows up late for your meeting at a restaurant in Wisconsin.

> You: I thought you took a wrong turn and ended up in
> Canada or something.

> Friend: No, I was just following my GPS. It just took longer
> than I expected.

Like a mouse walking into a deadly mousetrap, your playful comment died the second it reached your literal friend. Let's give your friend another chance. Because "Canada" was the keyword this time, your friend incorporates something commonly associated with Canada:

> Friend: Maybe I did... that would explain all the *moose* I saw
> walking around!

During a book signing with comedian Andrew Tarvin, author of *Humor that Works* (Tarvin 2019), I thanked him for signing his new book for me. But instead of saying something predictable, I offered a sarcastic hypothetical comment, "Thank you so much, now it'll be worth more when I sell it on eBay." He knew I was joking, and he played along without skipping a beat, "Yeah, probably about 52 cents more!" Moments later, he continued, "I could pretend to sign it to Barack Obama if you want? Like, 'Hey Barack, thanks for being my number one fan.'" Andrew Tarvin knew how to continue the play like the pro that he is.

If you've been reading every chapter so far, you may remember the following example. We'll keep the fun going longer this time.

> Lisa: What should we order for lunch?

> Erin: I don't care, I'll eat anything... except for mushrooms.

Lisa: Oh yeah? Because I was thinking we could just go pick some morels in the field over there and have a picnic.

Erin: No thanks, where do you want to eat for real?

On second thought, we can't keep the fun going because overly serious Erin crushed the playfulness with her *cold, mushroom-hating hands!* Let's give Erin another shot at it and see what happens if she decides to play along:

Erin: Could we? That would be the best lunch ever. And we could look for truffles too while we're at it!

Lisa: Great idea, I'll go rent a few pigs to help us find them.

Erin: And I'll bring bread for mushroom sandwiches. This will be the greatest feast of my lifetime. I can't wait.

Bravo Erin!

One time at work, I was sitting at my desk when a new employee was introduced to me by my friend Rick. (Side note for everyone starting a new job: they will be looking to see if you can play along with others.) In this case, Rick decided to be sarcastic and utterly understate my role to that of a lowly intern: "This is Greg, he's the guy who typed your name into the New Employee Welcome kit." The new employee caught on to Rick's subtle joke and successfully played along, "Wow, I'm impressed, I don't have an easy name—that must have been hard work." Do you think I played along? You're darn right I did! "Yeah, it took a few days... I had to stay all weekend to get it done." The new employee adapted quickly and hit the ball back in my court, "I hope you didn't hurt yourself." I responded, "I went through a few Band-Aids, but I got it done." I knew the new guy would do just fine at my company after that one interaction.

If the new employee didn't know how to play along, the entire lighthearted interaction would have been stopped dead in its tracks and we would have all had a different (worse) impression of the new guy (who did have a ridiculously long name by the way).

It's not always necessary to agree in order to keep the ball rolling. Remember the yoga example from earlier in the book? Let's revisit it one more time:

Jay: What are you doing?

Joyce: I'm doing my yoga. This is called 'downward-facing dog.'

Jay: It looks more like the 'distressed dog' to me!

Joyce: What's your pose called? *Reclining Sloth?*

Jay: Very funny. No it's actually called *Waiting for Cake.*

Joyce: Do you know the more advanced *Waiting for Cake and Coffee?*

Jay: As a matter of fact, I was hoping you could teach me that one.

Joyce: As soon as I'm finished with my yoga...

Remember, even if you can't think of a response; you usually have the option of responding in a way that keeps the play going. If you initially respond with comments like, "Yeah, you never know...," or "Maybe...," or "I just might...," you'll buy yourself more time to think of a way to keep things going. Even if you can't think of anything on the spot, it keeps the play alive for someone else to continue in the meantime.

What if the Only Logical Answer is 'No'?

Sometimes you're asked questions where the only possible answer you can think of is "No." Of course, the drawback to "No" is that it potentially stops the conversation dead in its tracks.

What if someone asks if you own a boat, but you don't? You could feel inclined to kill the conversation with a "No," but I challenge you to think more playfully. You could sarcastically answer affirmatively, "Yeah, I have about three boats... but they're plastic and only go in the bath tub." What hypotheticals could you mention if you did own a boat? What kind would it be? How much would it cost? Where would you go? What would you name it? Use your imagination! Remember the hypothetical for those moments when you become stuck. Look at what occurs in the following example:

> Friend: Do you have any cookies left?
>
> You: No.

That's all folks! Or is it? What if you added a hypothetical?

> You: If I did, I would probably be stuffing my face with them right now!

Much better! Let's look at another example. You visit a friend's home.

> Friend: Want some coffee?
>
> You: No, thank you.

Just responding with "No, thank you," puts up a "No" barricade to any additional (and lighthearted) conversation. Before giving up, try thinking of a hypothetical.

You: No, thank you. Coffee has a powerful effect on me. I might start bouncing off the walls.

Friend: Yeah, me too! I'm so sensitive to caffeine. This one time I drank like four cups before I had to deliver a presentation and...

Homework

Pretend for a moment we're talking, and I ask you, "Do you own any exotic pets?"

How would you respond? What if I also ask, "Do you own any weapons?" Initially you may answer "No" to both of my questions. Instead, try answering with one of the following structures:

No. If I did, I would/wouldn't _____.

No. If I did, I could/couldn't _____.

Technique #27

Use the Meta, Luke

If there was a universally powerful force in the conversation world, it would be meta comments.

Real–life Example

Think about the last time you heard a presentation at a formal event. Do you remember how the speaker started? Probably something like this: "How is everyone doing tonight?" You may recall what happens next. If the speaker is experienced, they often employ one of the most used meta-lines of all time: "Is that all you've got, you can do better than that!" Or similarly, "I didn't hear you, let me try again, HOW IS EVERYONE DOING TONIGHT?"

Why It Works

Instead of addressing what the audience said, the speaker commented on *how* the audience said it. Experienced speakers know they can comment *about* the audience's response. Listen for it next time. Try it yourself if you're delivering a message at a special event to a large group of kids, adults, it doesn't matter really. It works. Every time. If the speaker doesn't get a good reaction to a joke, he may say, "Oh, tough crowd."

The meta comment, like the force in Star Wars, exists outside the world of ordinary comments. Meta comments are statements *about* the conversational interactions, people, and scenarios themselves, as if you're outside of everything, just observing.

The prefix "meta" historically means "about the thing itself." You can theoretically employ them anywhere there's communication happening. They are useful in group banter, initiating conversations, recovering from mistakes, defending against verbal attacks, humor, and much, much more.

Let's look at a more conversational example of meta comments occurring between a group of friends.

Fran: Hot Pockets would be perfect in that situation.

Pat: Weren't we just talking about Hot Pockets like ten minutes ago? I was hoping to steer us away from anything related to Hot Pockets. Let me know when we're done.

Randal: Actually, I'm going to make it my goal to always reference Hot Pockets at least once in every conversation from now on.

Fran: Then my goal is to avoid talking with Randal for as long as possible.

What was particularly special about that interaction? They referenced the social interaction itself in some way.

I attended a meeting at my company recently, and the guy running the meeting needed to show us the new application he helped design. Although he was shy and somewhat quiet, was very funny. How did he pull it off? He had mastered the use of meta comments. The way he kicked off the presentation was a brilliant use of meta: "Normally Samantha does this demo, so I apologize that you guys are stuck with me. I'll try to act like Samantha as much as possible." Later, his date of birth appeared on the screen as he demonstrated a feature that asked for his age. He nonchalantly stated, "That's my actual date of birth... feel free to send me a card or a gift. I'm really into drones at the moment."

There are a ton of different types of meta comments, so I figured I'd do you a favor and group them into the following hopefully-not-too-confusing categories: *Actions, Voices, Words and Internal Thoughts.* In my experience, meta comments are one of the fastest and simplest routes to obtaining a laugh or a smile. And unlike many types of humor techniques, they carry minimal risk.

Comment on Actions

> Did you really just add water to your coffee? I'm going to pretend like I didn't see that.
>
> I probably should have held the door for you just then...
>
> Is this the point where you're supposed to ask me out?
>
> Did you just do the *come-hither* gesture?
>
> Did you like how I just invited myself to go to lunch with you? I'm pushy like that. I hope you don't mind!
>
> I totally just did the finger point at you.
>
> This is the point where it would be really romantic if you leaned in and kissed me.
>
> We just had a special moment right there. I'm not sure we'll ever have a moment like that again. Let's cherish it. I'm already looking back on it fondly.
>
> Do you like how I just stared blankly instead of responding? Sorry! I didn't mean to. I was lost in thought!

Comment on Voices

> Did my voice just crackle? Maybe I'm still going through puberty.

Pat almost did a full laugh there. It was kind of like a baby laugh or a half laugh.

Did I sound like a teacher just then?

Comment on Words

Nice tie by the way. I figured I'd start with a compliment before I asked you a favor.

You can make anything sound perverted, can't you?

Was that a real laugh or a pity laugh?

That sounds like a beauty pageant question.

Did you like how I added the part about chickens in there? I was hoping you'd notice.

Kenny: Are you actually having a conversation about leg sweat?

Steph: Yes.

Kenny: Okay. Just checking. I'll be going back to work now.

Co-worker 1: Inputting Excel data *is fun isn't it?*

Co-worker 2: Sure! 'Fun' for some people. I'd use a different word.

Comment on Internal Thoughts/Feelings/Intentions

I purposely decided to wear my argyle sweater so you would think I have an eccentric sense of style.

I was hoping I would get here earlier so you wouldn't think I was a perpetually late person, but I guess I blew that idea huh?!

I'm just being dramatic, hoping people feel sorry for me.

Well, that makes sense! I was sitting over here wondering, 'where is everybody?'

This really hurts. I probably shouldn't have skipped yoga class this morning!

Why do I feel like I'm in a meeting right now?

Why do I feel like I'm being interrogated right now?

I didn't want to stand around by myself, so I figured I'd come and introduce myself.

I know what you're thinking... this guy is a musical genius. But I'm really not, it's all an act.

Wait! That wasn't supposed to happen on that slide. I know what you're thinking—but believe it or not I have actually used PowerPoint before.

Many meta comments about conversation can help you *initiate* conversation. It's not uncommon for business people to preface a general comment with a meta comment, like the following:

I guess I'm supposed to say something about _____.

You may call me crazy for saying this, but...

You'd probably shoot me if I didn't at least mention _____.

Meta comments won't typically result in an eruption of laughter, but there is a high probability of achieving a smile or two, and that's the start of something fun.

I was in a project meeting at work one time where we were all asked to draw a picture and show it to everyone in the meeting.

The drawings all ranged from silly to scary, but it was the way everyone shared their drawings that got my attention. Everyone introduced their drawings in a different way. See if you notice anything interesting about the following examples:

Bill: This is my drawing. It has a large circle here, and...

Gill: I apologize if this creeps anyone out, but I drew a...

Dan: I may have gone a little crazy on the number of spikes...

Fran: Dear Lord, how am I supposed to follow that? I only drew a circle...

Stan: Just a warning, I draw at a third grade level...

Zan: If he draws at a third grade level, then I draw at a kindergarten level...

Out of everyone above, who do you think incited the group to laugh? Actually, they actually all received a degree of laughter except for poor Bill, he stuck with the literal introduction to his drawing. Everyone else kicked off their presentation with some good old fashion meta phrases.

Spin Mistakes into Humor Gold

I'm guessing you're human. Am I right? I knew that because I'm a really good guesser. You were created with a unique feature: *you make mistakes.* Even perfect Mary Lou from tenth grade who always got straight As and dated all the popular guys made mistakes. If you aim for perfection, you'll never be happy.

There will be plenty of times where you make a blatant error and wish to recover or move on from it. Meta comments are inherently effective at recovering from awkward situations. Verbal mistakes are like snowballs—if you act like they bother you, they grow bigger (and more threatening). Meta comments are your best bet for quickly deflecting any potential negative barbs, adding some levity, and moving the conversation forward. A few examples:

> That was my 'duh' moment for the day. Hopefully there aren't any more coming.

> I was cycling through every smart thought I had, but nothing came out except for that! Anyway, I need more coffee... or sleep. Or probably both.

> What just came out of my mouth? *Did I really just say that?*

Even if the mistake was not awkward at all, highlighting it with a meta comment can be entertaining conversation material. If you admit the mistake first, you can sometimes take advantage of it and spin the awkward straw into humor gold.

> That was a horrible analogy! Can I take that back, I don't know how that happened, it just kind of slipped. Strike it from the record, please.

We Were All Thinking It Anyway

Underpinning a lot of meta comments is a matter of simply bringing to the surface what people are thinking in a particular situation. Reread the first example from the *Comment on Action* category: "Did you really just add water to your coffee? I'm going to pretend like I didn't see that." The person who made that comment was probably thinking that thought while watching a guy pouring water into his coffee. And the guy pouring the water into the coffee probably understood that it's not a popular behavior and may have looked weird to other coffee drinkers. The person may even have thought to himself, "This probably looks weird... I hope no one notices." Saying that thought aloud, like, "I know this looks weird, I was hoping no one would notice," or, "This is going to look bizarre, you may want to look away," serve as good meta comments too!

Technique #28
Follow Up with a Meta Afterthought
Failed to say anything funny? Take one more (meta) shot.

Real-life Examples

Mike tells a colleague about his weekend plans.

> I'm thinking of going by myself to see the re-release of *Titanic* this Saturday afternoon.

Mike could stop there, but check out how much more dynamic his comments become when followed up with a meta afterthought:

> ...it might be the loneliest afternoon ever.

> ...I can tell that you're jealous. You thought about going too, didn't you?

> ...I guess I'm just a glutton for punishment.

> ...how big of a loser am I?

> ...I would do anything for Leonardo DiCaprio, okay?

Why It Works

Sometimes your initial comments aren't funny, and that's okay. The meta afterthought offers one more opportunity for an injection of playfulness. Think back on all of the previous categories of meta comments, the meta afterthought is follow-up commentary about something you (or someone else) just did or said. For example, state a possible consequence or reaction to what you just did or said. Reflect on it. Think about any underlying, unstated premises or subtexts of the initial comment and say them out loud. In the previous example, going to watch a sad romantic drama by oneself on a Saturday afternoon has a few different

163

possible premises, each addressed by one of the aforementioned examples of meta afterthought.

A colleague tells you how to do something you've already experienced, and you respond, "Don't worry, it's not my first rodeo." Nothing funny so far, however, what possibly sticks out in your response? Not a lot of people throw around the word *rodeo* every day. If something seems a little different than the norm, you have a perfect opportunity to say something about it. In this case, leverage a meta afterthought to do just that:

...see what I did there? I used a cowboy idiom.

...I always wanted to say that.

...and I don't even like cows or cowboys.

As you hopefully already learned from the previous chapter, meta afterthoughts can be as simple as "...well that was embarrassing." Let's look at some additional examples:

Initial Comment: I just a bought a tuna sandwich from a gas station.

Meta Afterthought: ...I know, I like to live dangerously.

Initial Comment: I found the coolest thing ever—scented candles that smell like bacon and pancakes.

Meta Afterthought: ...It's the perfect invention. We should just stop trying to invent anything else.

Initial Comment: I'm going to do _____.

Meta Afterthought: ...because I'm a loser/badass/nerd like that.

Conclusions, Summaries, and Realizations, Oh My!

Meta afterthoughts in the form of a *conclusion, summary,* or *realization* work well. For example: "So yeah, hitting a hornets' nest during a soccer game probably wasn't the best idea I've ever had..." Check out a few examples below:

> I have no idea how I ate the entire thing, but now I'm paying for it.
>
> So, stay away from Jack when's he's hungry, is the moral of the story.
>
> I'll never be doing that again.
>
> I probably shouldn't call people at 3am anymore.

Meta afterthoughts can help shape the other person's response. And they can help the conversation playfully flow by ensuring your conversation partner stays involved. Check out these examples:

> Am I just being paranoid, or is that not weird?
>
> Do you see what I mean? He's crazy, right?
>
> I know I was rambling there. Did that make sense?
>
> Who does that? Who brings an entire uncooked salmon to someone's house?

Although I've attempted to avoid a lot of technical comedy jargon, sometimes I can't help myself. A "callback" is the act of drawing a humorous connection between the present topic and a previous topic—preferably within the same conversation. For example, if I was admitting how I get out of awkward situations by pretending my back hurts, and later in the conversation someone playfully complains, "Oh my back is hurting, I think I need to go," that would be a funny callback to what was previously discussed.

The participants of the conversation would understand the subtext, even though it wasn't outwardly stated.

I witnessed a perfect example of a meta afterthought callback during lunch with colleagues recently. The small talk centered on the show The Bachelor (ABC 2018). Joe said, "The Bachelor is lame this year, I think the whole thing about him being a virgin is overrated." Later in the conversation, we were talking about weird human habits. Joe said, "What about those people who close their eyes while they talk? How weird is that?" Megan pounced on the opportunity to summarize and form a conclusion based on a few disconnected parts, "Well, it's official, now we know Joe hates closed-eyed virgins!" Megan's comment resulted in a raucous round of laughter. Even comedy legends Conan and Aziz would have been impressed with that one.

Technique #29

Tap into Your Keg of Pop Culture Knowledge

If you're like the average American, you probably possess a giant mental storage tank of refreshing pop culture references; start using your knowledge for humor.

Real-life Examples

One time, my friend busted out a few dance moves while at work. Remarking, "You're pretty good" or "You could use some practice," wouldn't win me any comedy awards for best one-liner. But what if I incorporate pop culture references in my comment instead? My responses may sound like one of these:

> I'm impressed; you could be the next *Lord of the Dance.*

> Wow, Michael Flatley's got nothing on you!

> You're giving Michael Flatley a run for his money! You could have your own *Lord of the Dance* tour.

> You're like Michael Flatley, but with longer hair.

Similarly, my friend could make additional references:

> I'm no Michael Flatley, but...

> I know I'm amazing. Michael Flatley couldn't even keep up with these legs!

> I should start my own *Lord of the Dance* tour!

Why It Works

Did you find those Michael Flatley comments funny? If you didn't, you may not be familiar with Michael Flatley. And that's the risk that comes with pop culture references, and why they are a more advanced comedic technique. It's important to tailor your references to your specific audience. I don't know anything about you, so I'm just taking a stab in the dark with any reference I make throughout this book.

Would you prefer I referenced Usher or Drake instead of Michael Flatley? Well, you're in luck! Conveniently, if my friend was attempting to sing, hum a tune, or anything else music related, I could sarcastically reference either of those two performers:

> You sound just like Usher; I could barely tell the difference.
>
> You're like the skinny nerdy version of Drake.
>
> You remind me of Usher, except without the good voice or dance moves.
>
> You remind me of Usher, except with much better dance moves.

People love making pop culture references. Some people by reciting quotes or acting like famous movie characters. It's a wonderful bonding activity and a super way to demonstrate similarities. I can't tell you how many times I got an instant chuckle from simply quoting Inigo Montoya from the movie *The Princess Bride* (Rob Reiner 1987) "You keep using that word... I do not think it means what you think it means," in the middle of a conversation. I don't always quote famous characters, but when I do, I quote Inigo Montoya. (Did that last line sound familiar? You may have recognized that it sounded similar to the catch phrase used by *The Most Interesting Man in the World* from the Dos Equis commercials, circa 2010). Almost every adult in America was familiar with that commercial at one point. Modifying it to fit a different context can be pretty funny. At dinner, I could apply it in a slightly different way, "I don't always drink soda, but when I do, I drink Dr. Pepper."

Anyway, let's look at another example, because although I'm not the Lord of the Dance, I *am Lord of the Examples.*

My family was going through a spate of sicknesses over the past few weeks. I was describing our experience to a friend and they remarked, "It's like you're on the *Oregon Trail* or something! Maureen has come down with typhoid fever. Rowan has dysentery..." We had a good laugh over that reference because we both loved that game as teenagers.

Your references should vary between direct and subtle, depending on the level of understanding your audience has. The British culture is a fitting example of a culture containing many easy-to-reference themes and stereotypes for my friends and me. For instance, one time we were getting coffee, and one of my friends said:

> Starbucks just raised their prices, so I'm only buying *tea* from now on.

I drew upon our common understanding that the British are famous tea-lovers.

> You sound like you've just turned British!

There was no disguising the stereotype—it was just stated. But my friend understands the nuances of British culture, so at some point I also alluded to the stereotype:

> Do you want crumpets too? Or some little cucumber sandwiches?

Let's look at another example. You're touring a building with a group of people and you lose one of the people in the group. What similar scenario from a popular movie comes to mind? How about *Willy Wonka and the Chocolate Factory?* "I feel like we're in Willy Wonka's factory right now where one of us is going to disappear at every turn." Check out some others (many of which could be applied to numerous situations):

> That was horrible! I need one of those *Men in Black* memory sticks to erase my memory now.

> I'll just be your *Vanna White* over here. You let me know when I need to change it again.

> Mark was making some good arguments. He was throwing left and right hooks, throwing haymakers, but then *Apollo Creed* snuck in and popped him in the jaw.

> You need it finished by Friday? Who does he think you are, *J.K. Rowling*? You can't write that quickly!

Of course, one of the best parts about a reference is that it opens the door up to more playful conversation. If someone else understands the reference, they're likely to play along. If you reference a movie scene, it's not unusual for anyone familiar with the scene to recite a quote from one of the characters. Make sure you try to play along too if you can!

I was listening to a podcast (Conan O'Brien Needs a Friend, with Hannah Gadsby, 2019) where Conan was talking about his travels to Australia. "There are all these rules...this is the district you're in..." And as soon as he said the word "district," it triggered a reference by his guest, Hannah Gadsby. "*District*? Did you visit *The Hunger Games* by mistake?" Conan instantly understood the movie reference and without skipping a beat replied, "Yeah, it was weird, it was a long train and Woody Harrelson was there." Which, if you've seen the movie, you understand that Conan perfectly played along with the movie reference.

Justin and Melissa are having a fun conversation about the movie *Top Gun*. Because of their *knowledge* of the movie, they pulled off three separate Top Gun references within this brief interaction:

Melissa: You hear Top Gun is going to be in 3D?

Justin: Really? Those air combat scenes should be sweet.

Melissa: I'm probably not going to watch it.

Justin: What? I thought for sure you would watch it—you're like the Queen of 80s movies; how can you not like Tom Cruise singing *You've Lost that Loving Feeling.*

Melissa: Slow down there, *Iceman.* I've never seen you get so excited over a movie before.

Without existing knowledge about the movie, the conversation might have proceeded as follows:

Melissa: You hear Top Gun is going to be in 3D?

Justin: Yeah? It's been a while since I saw it—I don't really remember it.

Melissa: Oh, well—you might like it.

Justin: Yeah, maybe.

Millions of conversations a day meet a similar boring fate because one or both of the conversation partners can't (or won't) contribute more information.

Pop Culture Not Your Thing?

If you're one of those people who has a tough time remembering movie characters or other pop-culture references (or you just don't care to remember), you're in luck. Focus your efforts on making references to real-life scenarios, common experiences, events, or human behaviors instead. Most of us have experienced or are familiar with hundreds of commonly understood events that make good reference material. For example:

Christy walks into a zoo with her boyfriend, Patrick, and is surprised by all the flashing lights and loud music.

> Christy: Is this a zoo, *or a night club?*

> Patrick: I feel like I should start dancing right now!

Through personal experiences and observations, you probably know what it is like to:

- Stand in line at the DMV
- Attend a concert
- Get bullied in school
- Get pulled over by the police
- Have to share something with a sibling
- Have the first kiss with someone you like
- Go to the movies and eat popcorn
- Drive through a snowstorm

Any number of these experiences can make entertaining references of various kinds. Let's look at some more:

> You know how when you walk into the DMV and you draw number 172, and they're only on number 18—*that's how I feel right now.*

> I'm getting anxious. I mean, I'm not nervous like *getting pulled over by police* nervous, more like *driving through a snowstorm* nervous.

> It's kind of like when you wait all week to see a movie and it completely lets you down.

Some references are more subtle. Imagine you're visiting a friend at their house and they hand you a bottle of Coke to drink.

The standard response is, "Thanks." But you could be more playful and reference another type of drink someone offers a guest in a slightly different context.

Oh, it looks like it's a 2018—that was a good year.

When you open it, you could pretend to smell the cap.

This Coke has aged well.

Did you guess the reference? Of course, you did! Acting like the Coke was wine is applying well-known expressions/ideas from one context to another context.

For another cross-context example, you could use fancy legal jargon in a different context. Rather than saying "I think we should go to Chipotle," you could say, "I put in a formal request that we go to Chipotle." Someone may catch on to your act. "I second that." This normal situation is boosted by making it appear like you're participating in an official meeting or legal proceeding.

Recently my family was visiting my in-laws. My mother-in-law made breakfast for my eight-year-old son, Kaerigan. He yelled at her, "You burned my bagel, I don't want it now!" I made light of the awkward situation by saying, "Uh oh, grandma, looks like you're going to get a bad *Yelp review.*" She continued, "I know, no one's going to want Grandma's breakfasts anymore." We pretended to act like her house was a restaurant and my son was a customer. Instead of Yelp, I could have referenced Trip Advisor, Google Reviews, etc. The restaurant label and subsequent references were used many times throughout our vacation to good effect.

On the podcast, *Conan O'Brien Needs a Friend* (with Patton Oswalt, 2019) Conan's assistant mentioned that she's ¼ Greek. Conan and his staff latched onto that single unique attribute and hilariously referenced other common heritage-related scenarios. I'll summarize a few of them for you:

Do you ever go around saying, 'Kiss me I'm quarter Greek.'?

I think there's a quarter Greek parade tomorrow.

You wanna go get some quarter Greek food later?

There are endless sources of cross-context material if you look for them. You owe a friend a dollar for a coffee? Employ a common expression used for paying for larger items, "Do you take credit?" Your friend loves Taco Bell a little too much? Reference a well-known place people go for addictions: Maybe he needs *Taco Bell rehab.*

Technique #30
Label, Meet Reference

Labels are often funny on their own. But labels plus references are a match made in comedy heaven.

Real-life Examples

>Pat: My kids eat a lot of hummus.
>
>Randal: That's because you raise your kids like a hippy would. Did you hand-sew their clothes too?
>
>Pat: That's right. And I drive them to school in a Volkswagen Beetle—I don't think I could be any hippier if I tried.

Why It Works

In the first example, Randal introduced the hippy label, which could kick off endless comments related to how Pat acts like a hippy. Pat even played along. She may or may not drive a Beetle to school; it doesn't even matter because they were just playing around. What else do hippies do, eat, drive, or say? I'm sure you could think of more ways to continue playing with that label if you tried.

The beauty of labels and references is that they often *initiate* play. And of course, that's one of the themes of this book: incorporate more types of comments that push the conversation into the play zone. It's important to first create an environment for laughter if you want to make people laugh.

As a friendly reminder, labels, stereotypes, or generalizations work best when employed in a playful and innocuous manner with good friends because there's inherent risk with putting people in narrowly defined categories. Here are a few popular and usually lighthearted stereotypes: soccer moms, hippies, hipsters, hillbillies, rednecks, hunters, high school bullies, truckers, and dumb jocks. Anyone with extreme personality or physical traits work well too, for example: goths, people with face tattoos, body builders, guys with man buns, weirdos who write books about humor, and so on.

Let's look at another example. Tom and his friend Adam are at a bar and Tom orders Red Stripe beer. Adam and Tom understand that Red Stripe is a famous Jamaican beer, so Adam lobs a label at Tom and Tom plays with it.

> Adam: Oh, are you feeling Jamaican tonight?
>
> Tom: I loved Red Stripe back in my Jamaican phase. When I had long dreadlocks I drank it all the time.

The Label Summary

Summarizing another's statements helps to acknowledge that you're listening. But it's also an opportunity to apply a blanket generalization about something they said or did. Check out some examples to see what I mean:

> Sheila: They said I had a big butt—a bunch of the neighborhood kids were making comments.
>
> Randal: So, you're kind of like the *Kim Kardashian* of your neighborhood?
>
> Sheila: Yeah—except without the millions of dollars!

> Patrick: I got two numbers last night at the bar.
>
> Rick: Wow, so basically, you're a *pimp.*

Patrick: Yep, pretty much. I could teach you a few lessons in *pimp-ology* if you'd like—I won't charge much.

Continue It

When introducing a good theme or making an apt reference, the supporting example or detail can seal the deal. Additionally, if you hear someone else mention a good theme or reference, see where you can add a detail to theirs. Also, I've noticed that people may not always fully understand or appreciate your reference, *until* you include the supporting example or detail(s).

Mark: My wife always takes forever getting ready.

Mark's simple label is much more interesting when he includes a detail to support his observation and answers the question, "How so?" Check it out:

Mark: She has to put on seventy-two different products, brush her hair for 30 minutes, write in her journal, sniff through all fifteen perfumes... I could get a great power nap in with the time it takes her to get ready!

Let's look at another example. Dave talks to his friend Pete.

Dave: *How did you know that?* You know the most obscure things.

Dave introduced a label and then successfully supports it:

Dave: We should build a website and call it *AskPete.com.* You can just sit there all day in your PJs and answer everyone's questions.

Pete: That would be my dream. Except no one would be allowed to ask *sports* questions. There is a black hole in my brain where sports knowledge is supposed to live.

See how much more entertaining their conversation becomes? In the following example, Andy talks facetiously about his friend Jason.

Andy: I don't want to offend Jason—you know *he angers easily.*

You know the drill. Andy introduced a label; he should support the label.

Andy: If you're not careful, he'll be talking about you on Twitter at 2am.

Don't forget to add to labels about yourself. Check out this example where Joe does a nice job labeling himself and then adds to it in multiple ways:

Justin: It's not that complicated. I feel like you were thinking too deeply about it.

Joe: Yeah, but that's what I do. I'm a *deep thinker.* I can't help it. *I'm kind of like Aristotle.* I'm probably related to him.

Because Justin happened to know who Aristotle was, he was able to continue the reference with additional details.

Justin: That would explain your giant sandal collection.

Joe: How did you know about that? Let me know if you need any deep thinking later. I'm your man.

Justin: Okay, Aristotle. Don't let me disturb your theory of ethics or zoology or anything else you're working on.

Technique #31
Ask the Fun Questions
Some of the best questions are about hypothetical things that never occurred and never will.

Real-life Example

As Eileen walked toward her office, she noticed a coworker, Bob, coming out of the building, holding a computer monitor.

> Eileen: Hey Bob, what are you doing with that monitor?
>
> Bob: Oh, just taking it to another office.
>
> Eileen: Cool. Have a good day.

Wasn't that hilarious? Not so much. Nothing funny occurred there. If Eileen had a more playful mindset, what might she have asked instead?

> Eileen: Hey, *stealing office equipment again, huh?*
>
> Bob: You caught me! I'm selling monitors for just ten bucks—you interested?

Why It Works

As discussed back during all those techniques about hypothetical comments, some of the best and most entertaining comments revolve around topics, stories, and feelings that never occurred, nor ever will occur. Well, the same goes for posing questions. The most playful, funniest questions are often about imaginary, hypothetical things.

The reason I waited so long to review how to ask fun questions, is because some fun questions rely on everything you've learned up until this point: labels, references, sarcasm, premises, meta, and more, feeds into the making of fun questions.

First, let's look at an example of *what a fun question is not*. You probably already know about the Five Ws (who, what, when, where, and why) for seeking information. If you find yourself solely focusing on learning factual or literal information, you're probably not in the play zone. Funny people who ask fun questions don't necessarily care about seeking real answers right away, because, well, they value having fun too.

Jack: Where are we going on our date?

Jill: *It's a secret!*

Jack: Okay, but can you tell me where?

Did you hear that? That was the sound of Jack sucking the fun out of the conversation. His use of the "Where" question was strictly for seeking real info. Jill tried to make it fun, but Jack wasn't having it. Let's look at a different ending. This time, instead of asking a normal question, Jack plays along and asks a *fun question*.

Jack: It won't involve water or needles will it?

Of course, Jack isn't seeking real information with that question. But he knows that Jill will eventually tell him where they're going. By keeping the fun alive, the experience is much more playful.

This time, Jack, Jill, and some other friends are out for drinks. One of the friends mentioned how they just had dental work done, and Jack chimes in with his own experience.

Jack: Yeah. This tooth is actually fake. It's just a cap.

Jill: Really? I had no idea! This whole time I thought you had good teeth. *What else is fake?*

Jack: Actually, my entire face. I had brown eyes and black hair before the surgery.

Jill's question, "What else if fake?" was a perfect fun question because it opened the door for Jack or others to play along with the "fake/artificial" label. Jill clearly wasn't seeking real info, she was opening the door to the play zone instead.

Word Association

Your ability to ask good fun questions depends on how well you can spot keywords and draw entertaining connections to those keywords.

For example, Geoff's friend Rick moved to another city and they're talking about Rick's new apartment.

Rick: It's good, except I don't have any *hot water.*

Instead of relying on something boring, like, "Oh, that's not good," Geoff should try to make a connection to something or somewhere else lacking hot water. Maybe a forest? A third-world country?

Geoff: No hot water?! Where did you move to, *the back hills of Appalachia?*

Of course, the more familiar the person is with the reference, the funnier it will probably be.

Remember, if you're stuck in a serious mindset, you may not even pay attention to your brain when it delivers a fun or playful association. Those playful associations are the seeds for growing fun questions. Whether or not you take advantage of them is up to you!

Look at the following interaction:

> Will: How was your weekend?

> Bill: It was kinda *busy* actually.

> Will: Yeah, I hear ya.

But that wasn't funny. Will could have taken advantage of the keyword he was offered. And keywords are tricky things—they aren't always obvious. They don't come with flashing signs and neon lights. Check out what Will could have said if he had just explored the keyword "busy."

> Will: How was your weekend?

> Bill: It was kinda busy actually.

> Will: Good *busy* or bad *busy*? Like now you need to vacation on a tropical island *busy*?

Now that response has a much better chance of opening up some playful dialogue.

Here's another example. Geoff's friend Rick is describing his weekend plans.

> Rick: I'm going to *Atlanta* this weekend.

Okay, so what is associated with Atlanta? When you see that word, what do you think of? Gator shoes? BBQ? The TV series with Donald Glover? Check out how Geoff responded:

> Geoff: Cool, can you pick me up some nice gator shoes while you're down there?

Play with the Premise

Remember the humor technique about playing with the premise? (#20) Look out for possible underlying premises and refer to the opposite end of the premise spectrum with your question.

Your friend Andy talks about how he was traveling with the school band. What is a common stereotype in reference to *school band* members? When I mention the words "school band members," what comes to mind? They are perceived as well-behaved, nerdy types, right? (Sorry band people—love you guys!) Your hypothetical will be funnier if it brings up a scenario where the band members do something uncharacteristic of the stereotype. For example: "You have to watch out for those crazy trumpet players. I bet they were trashing the hotel rooms, weren't they?"

Here's a perfect example showing how to play with the premise. Theresa tells Richard about an experience with her son:

> Theresa: So, I've been potty training my son—that's been an adventure!

The premise is that her son is probably around three-years-old—a typical potty-training age—so Richard should think about something on the opposite end of the premise spectrum (but still within the realm of possibility).

> Richard: I bet! How old is he now, *14?*

> Theresa: Yeah. It's taken us over a decade. He's *slightly* behind his peers.

Sarcastic Questions

Similar to asking questions along the premise spectrum, sarcasm states the opposite of what's "understood," providing a good format for fun questions.

Let's go back to that toddler, Ethan, who colored all over his parents' walls. When you walk into their house, you could state the obvious: "Looks like Ethan drew all over your wall," but that'd be boring, right? Let's try some good old-fashioned sarcasm.

> Hey, I like the new wall decorations... have you been watching a lot of Martha Stewart?
>
> Nice wall décor... what style is that? French modern?
>
> Does Home Depot sell those paint colors?

Here's another example: One of my colleagues works in human resources, and I saw him looking at a college website on his computer.

> Me: Hey, what are you up to?
>
> Rick: Just trying to get into the summer semester... this college's website sucks.

He didn't mention what class he was trying to get into, which opened up an opportunity for me to make a wild, sarcastic guess.

> Me: I didn't know you were taking classes—what are you trying to get into? *Pottery* or something?
>
> Rick: Yeah, how'd you know? I feel like there's a lack of HR-themed pottery in our organization.

We went back and forth a bit with lines like, "Clay expertise is the one thing missing from my resume..." and, "Once I become an expert at making bowls, I'm sure to finally get that manager position I've always wanted." It was playful fun. Almost as fun as using a pottery wheel for the first time!

References, Labels, and Stereotypes

You call your good ol' friend Patrick and he informs you that he just got back from working out at the gym. What fun question could you ask? Think about ways to connect to the topic. What stereotypes and references are associated with *working out*? What labels and exaggerations could you introduce?

You may be tempted to ask purely information-seeking questions like "How was it?" or "How long were you there?" Which is fine for standard small talk, but also try to start thinking beyond the fact-based inquiries. In this example, you could reference a gym stereotype like the following:

> Did you have to change next to any old naked guys?
>
> Did you have to work out next to smelly B.O. guy?
>
> Did you use the TurboMax3050 and get your lats ripped?

The questions may be facetious in nature, but they serve to let Patrick know that you're interested in both playing and hearing more about what happened. Patrick plays along:

> Patrick: No, I didn't get too close to smelly B.O. guy, thank goodness. There was a really stinky guy who tried coming over to my machines though. I started smelling eggs, so I got the hell out of there. I think he started following me, honestly.

A good question (even a rhetorical one) helps your partner make additional connections, which in turn, keeps the conversation flowing. By simply asking "How was it?" and stopping there, you aren't really helping your partner make any specific connections to the gym. Some people prefer questions that aren't so open-ended. It may take Patrick a few moments to think of something on his own. Patrick may not have worked out near smelly guy, but maybe he had a similar experience, or maybe in his past he worked out next to someone unusual, and your question could have mentally triggered that story for him.

Hypothetical Summaries and Conclusions

Summarize or conclude something in a more exaggerated or fantastical way than expected. For example, instead of just stopping at "Should we stay in tonight?" Try, "Should we stay in tonight, or should we go get wasted at a dive bar?" Let's look at a few examples:

Joseph is nervous about how Maureen, his boss, is going to react when she hears about a mistake he made on a project. Joseph decides to consult his co-worker, Elizabeth.

> Joseph: So, did you ever talk to Maureen about the project?
>
> Elizabeth: Yeah, I did. I think she was okay with it.
>
> Joseph: That's good.

If Joseph took a more *playful* approach, he may have followed up with a hypothetical question.

> Joseph: Was there swearing involved? Did she start throwing chairs at you?

Joseph was able to lighten the mood with a few fun questions. Let's look at a few more:

> Melissa: I finally got him to tell the truth.
>
> Justin: *Did you have to drug him first?*

Rowan: So, what do you do?

Liam: I'm a bankruptcy counselor.

Rowan: So, you can make all my debts go away? Cool! When can I schedule an appointment?

The Incredulous Question

When you question why something unusual exists or why someone acted in some strange way, it often sets up opportunities to ask hypotheticals that could explain the behavior. Check these out (hypotheticals are in *italics*):

Look at that jerk. Who the hell parks like that? *Are they trying to get their car keyed?* Because I'm thinking about it.

You look great—how come you never seem to age? *What kind of magic elixir are you drinking every night?*

That has to be a wig. No one has hair like that naturally, do they? *She probably went to the store and said, 'Listen, I need one of those He-man wigs from that 1980s cartoon, do you have any of those?'*

Who let's their grass grow that high? *Are they waiting for goats to show up to eat it?*

Apparently a 95-year-old woman shot her son. How is that even possible? *Did her son have to stand still for ten minutes so his mom could figure out how to aim the gun?* And what would possess her to shoot him now after all these years? *Was she pissed that he overcooked her oatmeal that morning?*

Section 5

Tell Stories

Technique #32
Tell More Ten-Second Stories
You want to be funnier and more entertaining? Master the short story.

Real-life Examples

Willy and Billy did the exact same things this past weekend, but if you asked them each the question: "Hey, what did you do this weekend?" you'd hear completely different stories:

> Billy: Well, Saturday morning, I got up, ate some cereal, and then went to Home Depot to buy some tools. I bought a 5-bolt lock wrench and a few more ¾-inch bolts and I got back around 11am and worked on my Chevy until about 5pm. It needs a lot of work, especially the engine. There was a ton of carbon build-up, but it's an older car so that's how it goes sometimes. I didn't get very far before I decided to call it a day and have dinner. That's about it though, nothing too special.

> Willy: Well, Saturday was *car day*. I spent like 15 hours working on my old Chevy. I think my hands are permanently stained black from all the grease and oil. I swear that ol' car is going to be the death of me! I think I need to find a new hobby.

Why It Works

Billy and Willy epitomize opposite methods of storytelling. Billy's storytelling strategy is to cover the *facts*, whereas Willy leans more *playful*.

Why was Willy's story better? Willy called Saturday his "car day," making a label out of an ordinary day. He exaggerated the number of hours he worked on the car. He focused only on the interesting parts instead of the dry, technical details about wrenches and bolts and carbon build-up. He applied an exaggerated description to the stains on his hands and included a conclusion about how the car is going to kill him, and a meta afterthought about how he needs a new hobby. All classic humor techniques we've covered so far. Willy knew that his audience probably didn't care about the specific tools he bought at Home Depot. His entire story was more focused on emotions than facts.

Retelling what you did over the weekend is storytelling. Stories don't have to be elaborate tales of adventure, romance, and intrigue, where people gather around and listen to you for twenty minutes around a campfire. No one expects you to be a TED speaker or storyteller from The Moth. In fact, Willy's story was not particularly complicated, adventurous, or long.

Look at the following two versions of the same observation:

1. There was this guy on the street yelling something at my wife.

2. There was this old shirtless guy wearing a pair of Detroit Lions sweatpants, yelling something about his Snickers bar at my wife.

In this case, the more detailed version is more interesting, isn't it? The second example is more vivid and does a better job painting the scene, which helps the listener better imagine what's happening. Painting a more accurate picture also lends itself to better follow-up comments. For example, "Was this guy obsessed with Snickers bars or something?" Or, "Your wife should have been like, 'I don't even like Snickers bars! Leave me alone.'"

Details make the story more engrossing. Of course, the trick is to add just enough details to make the story colorful and captivating to the listener, but not so many that the story gets bogged down in unnecessary information, like with Billy's story. Only include details your listeners may be interested in hearing about. Having said that, there are some auto engineers and car enthusiasts out there who may have preferred Billy's story over Willy's!

Could You Elaborate Please?

So why ten-second stories? Why not forty-second or five-minute stories? Well, the thought of telling stories is intimidating for most people. You're not the only one who shudders at the thought of being the center of attention for too long. But I figure most people can handle telling a story for less than 10 seconds.

Of course, stories don't need to start with "Let me tell you a story." No, in fact, they're better when they spring up organically and within the flow of the conversation.

The best stories sprout from one primary habit: supporting your opinions and self-disclosure with *examples*—basically, just elaborate more. Start a habit of supporting what you say by talking about interesting experiences (even if it only takes up a few more seconds), and you'll be a regular storyteller without even realizing it!

Let's take a look at a before-and-after example of providing supporting anecdotes. You're having a conversation with Jan. Jan discloses the following information about her daughter throughout the chit-chat:

My daughter loves ice cream.

My daughter really likes dresses.

You learned that Jan's daughter loves ice cream and dresses. Cool. But Jan could have made the conversation more fun by elaborating on those facts. She never offered an *example to support how much* her daughter loves ice cream and dresses. If she did, the conversation would have been much more entertaining and enjoyable, and sounded more like this:

> My daughter *loves* ice cream... The other day we were at the grocery store and my daughter says, 'Mommy, *can we get some pumpkin ice cream? Can we get some pumpkin ice cream pleeeeease?*' I mean, she started this when we pulled into the parking lot and didn't stop until I was in the check-out line! I may need to get her professional help.

> My daughter really likes dresses. She's in that *only-wear-dresses phase.* She'll wear nothing else; she even wants to wear dresses instead of pajamas at bedtime! The more ruffles and bows, the better.

A good story usually points to elements of life that are unique, unusual, or interesting. Everyday life is full of events and occurances that make for interesting stories. (Read Techniques #7, 8, and 22 if you need inspiration for how to turn the mundane into entertainment.) Your stories might not land you an invitation to speak at a The Moth storytelling event, but that's okay. Unfortunately, many people hesitate to add any embellishments when they have the chance. (I'm definitely guilty!) As long as no one is in a hurry, you might as well throw in some additional support for your opinion or comment and see what happens. If your listeners are interested, they'll ask for even more!

I'm just not that interesting, you might be thinking to yourself. Well, I have news for you: any story about your experiences will be relevant and at least a little entertaining to your friends. Your friends and family care about you, so your stories are more likely to be engaging to them, even if it's just a story about how you dropped peanut butter on your pants this morning. I bet you have a few friends who would find that mildly amusing to hear about.

The key is to be enthusiastic about the story. This is incredibly important to remember: If you act like it's *not interesting*, then why would you expect anyone else to be *interested*? The way you tell the story is equally as important as what you're saying. I know a guy from France, named Jacque, who I seriously can barely understand because his accent is so thick and his grasp of English leaves much to be desired. However, because he's so passionate and enthusiastic about what he's saying, he still manages to captivate and entertain his listeners. If you're fluent in English, you're already one step ahead of Jacque!

Not only are stories socially entertaining, but they also allow you to share information about yourself and let others get to know more about you, your thoughts, feelings, and experiences. Don't hold back because you don't feel confident telling stories. It's not just about trying to entertain—think of storytelling as an act of *sharing more information*. When you make concerted efforts to share information; you will, at times, end up telling a story, even before you realize it!

Want more motivation to tell stories? How about this little nugget: the more someone knows about you, the more they tend to like you. (Unless, of course, you share something psychotic and disgusting—like your love of mushrooms or something). The more someone knows about you, the easier it becomes to talk to you. *Think about that for a second.* The more they know about you, the more comfortable they'll be at telling their own stories when they're with you. You'll be able to bond with people on a deeper level.

The Basic Story Structure

The majority of good stories are structured as elongated contrasts, where something normal eventually clashes with something unexpected. But unlike the contrasts we looked at up until this point, stories contain more detail, more build-up, and more explanation. Consider the following example where the storyteller sets up a normal scene, talks about how it won't rain, and then it does rain and ruins everything.

> I put both mattresses on top of the car. I'm like, 'No way is it going to rain today; there's not a cloud in the sky.' And of course, an hour later, as soon as we start driving, *WOOOOOOOSH,* rain starts pouring down out of nowhere! I was like, 'You gotta be kidding me!' They were both drenched. I'm never doing that again.

Even if your listener predicted the outcome of your story—it can still be interesting and entertaining if you infuse some enthusiasm into your words.

A good storyteller teleports listeners to a place where they can feel and experience something just as the storyteller experienced it. Telling parts of your story in the *present tense* helps you do just that. Here's part of a story told in the past tense: "And I stood there, I was next to a huge man, and then I looked at him, and I said to him, "Hey, do you mind moving?" Now let's teleport the listener directly into the scene by retelling the story in the present tense: "And I'm standing there, next to this huge man. I look him in the eye... "Hey, do you mind moving?"

Did you notice another difference between the two aforementioned versions? I've asked for advice from a number of professional storytellers. The consensus was that too many people overuse "he said," "she said," and "I said." Just get right to the dialogue. The context of the story is often enough for the audience to know who's saying what (unless it's too short or lacks enough details to know). Altering your voice slightly to match the character in your story helps too.

I've studied thousands of stories, and for the most part, they follow a similar pattern. I suggest memorizing the basic story structure now so your brain has less work later when you're on the spot.

The Five Parts of a Good Story

1. Paint the scene
2. Normalize
3. Contrast / Turning Point
4. Reaction
5. Conclusion / Meta Afterthought

You want to see all five parts in action? Okay, let's start with a simple but entertaining story:

> I'm at this dive bar, and I'm just ordering a Rum and Coke like normal, when suddenly this tall red-headed Irish guy pours his entire drink into my lap. I couldn't believe it! I'm like, 'What the hell's wrong with you?!' He stumbles away

into the crowd. He seems completely drunk. I'm not sure I'll ever go back there again.

Let's get a little dirty and take a peek under the hood. If I intentionally extract the story contents and leave only the structure, you'll notice the five story parts:

Paint the scene: I was at this _____.

Normalize: I'm just _____ like normal...

Contrast/Turning Point: When suddenly _____.

Reaction: I couldn't believe it! I was like, '_____!'

Conclusion/Meta Afterthought: He ended up _____. I'm
not sure I'll _____ again.

Paint the Scene

Help your listener imagine the scene before you talk about anything else. Set the stage and leverage a few descriptive and interesting details. It doesn't take much, but you shouldn't skip this part unless your listener is already familiar with the scene you're talking about.

So last week, I was driving to work on US-23, when it started
raining.

We were at the carnival, over in downtown Royal Oak, and
it was so crowded.

I'm sitting on my comfy recliner, watching TV, just minding
my own business.

Normalize

Establish a normal expectation so you can crash something against it later in your story. What were you expecting before the turning point in the story? What were your thoughts or feelings at that moment? Take the listener through your experience and your thought process. The better your normalizing is, the more entertaining the contrast and turning point will be.

> So, normally, I would just ask for my receipt, but _____.

> I was watching this movie and assumed it was going to be some boring chick flick.

> Normally I would have_____. I mean, I always _____, but I noticed that_____ so I _____.

> We were going to buy tickets from the main booth, and I was thinking it was going to cost $20 each, so we _____.

The Turning Point

There are many ways to phrase the turning point, but a common method is to mention *the moment in time* when the turning point (or some significant change) happened. A few turning point examples from real stories:

> He was standing in line; when all of a sudden, he leaned over and said _____.

> So, I finally pulled up to her house, and right as I stepped out of the car, out of nowhere came the _____.

> I just expected him to _____, *but instead he* _____.

And I was hoping that she was going to be working at her desk, *but then we walked in and you'll never believe what she was doing!*

And this is where everything breaks down. She says to me, '_____.'

It was that moment where I felt _____.

That's the moment where I was like _____!

The Reaction

In my experience, describing how I reacted typically triggers the best and biggest response from the audience. As a bonus, it's the easiest part to add—but sadly, novice story tellers rarely include the impact on themselves of what happened. If you can't fit in your own reaction, tell your listener how someone else reacted or felt about the event. People love hearing the human-interest elements of any story. They don't need a bunch of recited facts. They want something they can identify with emotionally. Include the reactions of the main characters in your story too.

After he said that, I was like '_____!'

After that, my mom just wanted to get out of there! You should have seen the look in her eyes!

My sister saw me and thought I was crazy! She was like '_____!'

I mean, I was in total shock. How could a three-year-old actually _____ on their own? It's almost unbelievable.

Oh my gosh, we were dying with laughter! My friend Jenny was practically rolling on the floor. I couldn't believe he said that! I was like, '_____!'

And then I took it back out—he probably thought I was a
complete moron at that point. He looked at me like I was
crazy.

Wrap it Up with Conclusions and Meta Afterthoughts

What happened after the turning point and reaction occurred?
What were the consequences? Now that you've had time to reflect,
how do you feel about what transpired?

> So, after he gave it to me, I just threw it into the crowd. And
> I never saw it again. I still can't believe he did that.

> And if it wasn't for Joe, I don't know where we'd be right
> now! *Probably stuck in a ditch somewhere.*

> I don't know how he ever got the job, but he made it
> somehow. I guess that goes to show you that nice guys do
> sometimes finish last.

> I should have just driven him home after he puked the first
> time. I don't know why I let him go back out there!

> I mean, how was I supposed to know there were going to be
> giant vampire flies?

> I almost died from embarrassment. I wanted to jump out
> the window after that! I still haven't been over there. I
> can't believe I did that.

Not sure how to finish strong? Remember to use superlatives;
they work great for tying a colorful bow around your story.

> And the worst part of the whole thing was _____.

> And the weirdest part of all was _____.

> The most ironic thing about what he said was _____.

I'll be honest, it was one of the best days of my life.

I mean, it was the strangest looking car I'll probably ever see.

After that, I felt like the biggest loser!

Now that you learned what goes into a good short story, it's important to note that all five parts aren't absolutely critical to every story. Experiment with different combinations of story parts and discover what works best for you.

I was recently at a wedding for one of my friends and I knew going in that I would run into many acquaintances. Social climatologists predicted a 100% chance of small talk. I came in armed with a story that happened to me recently. Everywhere I went, you better believe that story came with me. *I was socially armed.* I probably told the core of the story five times throughout the course of one evening! And it got better the more I told it. Some people even added to it. Either way, one good preassembled story contained a lot of value!

The more you tell and remember stories, the larger your story repertoire will grow, and the more likely you'll be able to tell them the right way at the right times. For example, when friends or acquaintances stop by your house, there's often an awkward period before the conversation really picks up. My wife and I were fortunate to have a cat named Bijou, who would always appear and aggressively lick and rub against the new guests. Why did that help me tell stories, you ask? Because I know an amazing story about the time we lent Bijou out to my in-laws so he could catch the bat flying around their living room. Anyway, it's a great story, and one I told every single time guests arrived because Bijou's appearance was the environmental trigger I needed to naturally transition into the story. The story naturally got better every time I told it too. Even though Bijou died many years ago, he still lives on in the stories I tell. RIP Bijou.

Still Don't Have a Story to Tell?

Here's some good news: some of the best stories I've told have been other people's stories. Let me explain. I like to listen to a podcast called *Criminal* (Radiolab, 2019), and I was telling someone about one of the episodes. It involved a guy who hijacked a plane, lost all the money, ended up in jail, met an escape artist, nearly escaped again, and... anyway, it was a great true story. Of course, it wasn't my story—and it didn't matter. I told it to a friend, who was thoroughly entertained. The conversation with my friend started with, "I've been listening to the Criminal podcast, have you heard of it?" He hadn't listened to it, so I entertained him with the hijacking story. A week later, my friend told me that he shared my story with a few other people and they loved it. It had officially become *my story.*

Is your Uncle Larry doing some interesting things? What about your friend, Joe? Tell one of their stories. There are no laws against telling stories about other interesting people's escapades.

Homework

Now it's your turn. Pretend we're chatting. Tell me a story using the story structure you learned about in this chapter. If you're feeling ambitious, record yourself, and tell it a few more times, tweaking your lines, energy, and delivery a little each time until you've got an exceptional story. Practice your stories and keep them fresh in your mind for future use.

I'm going to also challenge you to tell a story about something that happened to you this past week—in fact, can you think of something right now? It's important to look for stories in the mundane and everyday experiences because they're certainly there: you just have to look hard enough.

Additionally, recent stories are typically more relevant and interesting than stories occurring in the distant past. Develop a habit of talking about events from the past week or so.

Technique #33
Commit to Character

Take advantage of the characters around you and bring them to life. If you never alter your voice, mannerisms, or energy level, you're handicapping your potential to be funny and entertaining.

Real-life Example

My wife noticed our normally tough-as-nails cat run back into the house on a cold snowy January day. She exclaimed, "You know it's cold out when Bijou runs out the back door and then runs right back in!"

That was a nice comment, but I left out the part that made it even better. She actually said: "You know it's cold out when Bijou runs out the back door and then runs right back in! He's like, "Aww HELL NO! *I don't think so!*"

Why It Works

I didn't laugh at my wife's comment until after she added the characterization and dialogue bit.

Robin Williams was one of my favorite comedians and I still love watching his old talk show appearances. If you study his acts, you realize that the secret to his success was his ability to get quickly into character. He had voices and mannerisms for hundreds of unique characters. Of course, you don't need to take it as far as he did, and few people could, but even *slightly* getting into character for any dialogue in your story or comment makes a dramatic difference.

Comedian Jim Gaffigan is famous for the character voice in his acts that portrays what the audience is thinking. He uses that voice as a foil, or reaction, to his jokes. More specifically, it's often the interior monologue of a stereotypical, middle-aged conservative woman reacting to his jokes. The reaction voice is sometimes the funniest part of his routine.

When you tell stories and describe what people are thinking, saying, or could say, it helps to differentiate the voices for characters so it's easier for the audience to follow along. Your voice doesn't have to change much at all for it to be noticeable and entertaining.

Dialogue helps bring your stories to life. Compare an old silent film to a modern movie. When you can hear the characters, you're more likely to be transported to their moment in the story; you're better able to share their experience. Look at the following versions of 10-second stories *without* and *with* character dialogue.

> Without: She wanted to wax my mustache—and I didn't even know I had a mustache. I was so traumatized—how come no one told me I had a mustache?

> With: She said in a thick accent, 'Do you want me to wax your mustache?' In shock, I was like, '*MUSTACHE! Yes please!*' I didn't even know I had a mustache! I was so traumatized—how come no one told me I had a mustache?

> Without: They started shouting at me every time I missed a goal.

> With: They started shouting at me every time I missed a goal—'*WHAT ARE YOU DOING, you idiot?!*' I was like, 'Are you really upset that I missed a goal during a practice? What's wrong with you?'

Without: I was so mad at him, I told him to leave!

With: I was so mad! I was like, 'Get the HELL out of my house, *you giant scumbag!*' And I wanted to say, '*And never come back!*' but I thought that might be too dramatic.

You have a license to embellish and exaggerate far beyond the literal and actual spoken words. Retelling what you or someone else said or thought is more entertaining when you exaggerate your impersonation of them (or your inner voice!). You don't need to go overboard; a subtle change in voice or mannerism is highly effective.

The best dialogue includes not only the factual recitation of events but the hypothetical possibilities:

- what you *wanted to say*
- what was *almost said*
- your thoughts/inner monologue
- what *should/could have been said*
- their hypothetical inner monologue

Years ago, I was in the middle of a park with my two-year-old, Rowan, when he looked up at me and said, "I gotta go potty; how are we going to *remedy* this situation?"

Admittedly, he was certainly not precocious enough to know the word "remedy," but it was fun to imagine him speaking so eloquently.

Have fun with imaginary phrases that you wished you (or someone else) had said at the time. Maybe you're describing some encounter with a jerk, "He was like '*Is there a problem?*' And I was like '*Yeah, there is a problem!* You're a big jerk and I hope I never have to talk to you again!'" Maybe you didn't say those exact words to him, but you wanted to, or thought about it. Don't leave that out—that's sometimes the best part!

One of my friends, Mike, told me a story about a recent shopping experience:

> We needed some new sheets, so I went to Target, and I decided to buy the fancy super deluxe 900-count sheets because I've never had sheets like that before. My wife was like, 'WHOA! I feel like I just teleported to a five-star hotel!'

Mike could have just concluded with, "...and my wife loved them," but he added some drama and entertainment with a fun quote from his wife instead.

Your inner dialogue is a fantastic medium for sarcastic humor. My friend, Andy, who is vehemently opposed to hunting, told a story about a hunting trip his father took him on when he was a child.

> That was the trip where I actually killed my first deer. My Dad was so proud. He ran up to me and said, 'Son, because you did so good, I'm gonna show you how to gut the deer.' I thought to myself, '*Oh boy, I can't wait!*'

The way Andy characterized and imitated his Dad, and then Andy's internal reaction to his Dad, took the story to the next level.

Homework

Watch some old clips of Robin Williams and Jim Gaffigan, and study thier ability to get into character. See the Recommended Viewing list for many more examples.

Bring Along a Side Comment

Batman was better with Robin. Help your main comment or story become more effective and entertaining by adding a side comment.

Real-life Examples

> So, he offered us drinks, but we told him we're not interested.

> And so, I was thinking, we should also plan the ski trip before January 10th. That would give us enough time to figure it out.

> After wrapping him up I almost dropped him. Anyway, so then I rocked him to sleep for an hour.

Did you spot anything entertaining in those examples? Not really? I didn't either. That's because they've been stripped of the original *side comments*. Now check out the examples with side comments (*in italics*) added back in, and imagine the side comments being spoken with a little extra pizzazz:

> So, he offered us drinks, *and you know how I am. I love a good martini,* but we told him we're not interested.

> And so, I was thinking, we should also plan the ski trip before January 10th. *I know, I'm crazy about timelines... my husband reminds me every week!* Anyway, that would give us enough time to figure it out.

> After wrapping him up I almost dropped him. *I'm such a horrible mom! I can't believe I almost did that!* Anyway, so then I rocked him to sleep for an hour.

Why It Works

Remember *meta afterthoughts* from Technique #28? The same "meta" principle is at work here. Side comments allow you and your audience to step outside of the story for a moment and elaborate or comment on elements within the story. Side comments are usually directed at yourself: how you're talking, acting, feeling, or some other observation.

These verbal asides can be light, fun, and unrelated to the story itself. They keep the audience engaged because they are unexpected and add a new dimension, all while buying additional time to think of where you're going next. Let's check out a ton more in action (again, the side comments are italicized):

> And I would have, but I was eating a hot dog, *because I like hot dogs and how could I turn down a hot dog at a ballgame?* So then_____.

> So, he leans over real close; *and you know I'm not a huggable guy. I like my personal space.* Then he says _____.

> And I gave it back, *even though the selfish part of me wanted to keep it.* But_____.

> And I was a little disappointed; because I was thinking there's going to be this delicious cherry pie, *which is my favorite by the way, in case you didn't know that or you want to buy me some,* but it wasn't even there!

> So, they lined up shots in front of us—*and you know when you have a shot in front of you, you have to drink it right? How could you not—it's bad manners if you don't.* I looked at the shots, and I looked at the bartender, and then....

> I finally saw him and just said '_____.' *I have no idea why I said that!* It just came out like that.

And I was thinking _____. *I don't know why; these are just the thoughts that go through my head!* So, I never actually did go through with it.

The best part is that you don't need to be witty to pull these off. None of them are particularly clever—yet they still often result in laughter.

Read the following story with and without the italicized side comments:

So I'm out for a run and notice there's an old, disheveled man on a bicycle following close behind me. Before I knew it, he caught up and started passing me! *So, I figured there was only one thing I could do at the moment—I raced him! I wasn't going to let an old guy on a bike beat me!* He started going really fast and I started sprinting next to him. And then...

Are you realizing the entertainment potential of side comments? Many side comments just explain your dilemma and voice what you're thinking at the time. Notice in the aforementioned example, if you leave out the side comments (*italicized*), and skip letting the audience into your inner thought process, the story is just a retelling of an event (certainly not as entertaining!) Here are a few more side comments that verbalize internal thoughts:

It was so awkward. I mean, what do you say to that?

I wasn't sure if we should buy him a drink or tell him to leave...

I didn't know if she wanted to go with me or stay there. I was so confused.

Remember the power of the hypothetical. Discuss what option you *should* have or *could* have chosen now that you have had time to think about it. Talk about what *almost* happened.

So, I just threw the ring back at him. I told him I was sick of dealing with his excuses every month. *I should have just kept it and sold it! That would have been a much better financial decision on my part.* I told him I was done.

She was so mad. *I expected her to grab my keyboard and throw it across the room!*

I was watching The Voice (ABC, 2019) the other night, and one of the judges, Blake Shelton, said, "If you plan to record The Voice and watch it later, *which I'm sure you will because it's the freakin' Voice*, then you'll see what I mean." It was his enthusiastic side comment that triggered the audience laughter. If he stuck to the basics, "If you plan to record The Voice and watch it later, then you'll see what I mean." It would have been a much more tepid audience reaction. So, if you apply the humor techniques in my book, *which I'm sure you will because everything in my book is freakin' awesome*, then you'll see how effective they are. See what I just did there? I'm so clever.

Side comments also help the audience connect to what you're saying. A key to engagement is to involve the people you're conversing with and avoid talking "at" someone for too long. Insert side comments like the following, which allow your listeners to better connect to the story.

Can you believe he did that?

I mean, is that normal? Have you ever done that?

Am I crazy for thinking that?

Don't fret if the story goes off the rails some—it's more important that the people listening are enjoying the experience, so go where the group wants to take it.

What about Stories Longer Than 10 Seconds?

Admittedly, some of the best stories are longer than 10 seconds. And when you start adding in all the story techniques, like *side comments*, it's easy to go beyond 10 seconds. When the mood and timing are right, feel free to elaborate further and shoot for long-form stories. Long-form storytelling is a more challenging skill, but one worth practicing over your lifetime.

Consider the following long-form stories and imagine them being told with gusto and enthusiasm. I took the liberty of including story part notations in the first story, but for the second story, you're on your own!

The Spider Story

My scariest spider encounter was when [paint the scene →] I was still living with my parents... and I walked into my room one time and my face hit a web... [side comment →] This wasn't a big deal because I was used to spiders in the house. And I'm normally cool with spiders, as long as they're not in the bathroom—then I'll kill them on the spot, but other than that it's all good. [normalize →] Anyway, I get to my desk and notice the web actually connects to my computer monitor. [side comment →] Which happens sometimes when the spiders get a little ambitious, which is fine. [turning point →] But this time, I turn on my computer light and I see the most horrific thing I've seen in years... Thousands of baby spiders are walking along the spider web! [re-emphasize turning point moment →] Literally thousands of spiders just hatched and are now all over my room! [reaction →] I was horrified! 'Are you frickin' kidding me? I'm outta here!' [conclusion] I don't think I went back in my room for like three days. I slept on the living room couch. [meta afterthought →] And I'm still deathly scared of spiders ever since that happened. I refuse to go see any Spiderman movies. Just kidding, Spiderman movies are awesome.

The Big Man and The Bus

One of the funniest stories I ever heard was about someone's experience sitting next to a large man on a bus. That's it. Nothing incredibly exciting or adventurous. And the storyteller could have just stated the basics, "A large man came and sat next to me on the bus, and it made me really uncomfortable." But instead, he elaborated on some of the finer details and painted the scene and his thoughts like a master storyteller. I heard this story nearly 20 years ago, but I still remember most of it as if it were yesterday—that's the incredible power of a good story. (Luckily, for the parts I couldn't recall, I saved all my notes.)

> Last week I was just riding a bus to work like normal, and there was a seat open next to me. Out of the corner of my eye, I saw this massive shape moving toward me. I honestly think the sun was blocked for a second. Anyway, I look over and I see him walking toward me. Well, it was more like he was scooting... yeah, scooting toward me. And I'm thinking to myself, 'Oh please no, oh please no... I'm claustrophobic, please don't sit next to me...I might freak out...' Now I'm a very accepting person and open to all people of all shapes and colors... but you know... he's probably 700 plus pounds

on a good day, but that's totally cool... except for when it comes to my seat on a bus. Sorry, but I need the room. I don't care. You probably think I'm a jerk... call me a 'bus jerk' if you want. So, then he leans over and asks if he can sit with me... Of course, I have to say 'Yes.' What was I supposed to do? This man could literally squish me if I angered him. I didn't want to risk my life... So, I said, 'Of course!' Well, needless to say, the rest of the ride was not the most comfortable in the world. *I became very intimate with the bus window* as I was squished against it. I think there's still a smudge mark on my face on that window... if you look for it you can probably still see it... So yeah, I think it's time I buy a car.

The storyteller not only followed a classic story structure, but loaded his story up with colorful descriptions, contrasts, labels, inner monologues, reactions, side comments, conclusions and meta comments. Did you spot any?

I admit, a story mocking someone's weight is not in the spirit of what I try to suggest throughout the book. (My editor was also not too pleased with this story!) As much as I encourage positivity, the truth is, a lot of humor involves painful, uncomfortable truths about the human condition. I have personally been the butt of many mean jokes over the years. One of the funniest targeted my horrible acne in high school. You want to hear it? Well, I'm happy to serve as your source of amusement! It started with one guy observing, "Greg has so much acne, we could play Connect the Dots with his face." To which another guy followed up with a brilliant barb, "I don't know, I don't even think Leonardo Da Vinci could connect *all those* dots!" Weren't those guys mean? Here's the reality: those guys were my best friends, and they're still my best friends to this day, more than 20 years later. Humor is complicated, isn't it?

I kept the bus story in the book because, regardless of how you feel about the subjects in the story, you can learn a great deal about long-form storytelling from that single story. In fact, if you memorized and rehearsed either of the previous two stories, you'd greatly enhance your ability to tell stories in general. Your brain would subconsciously learn the underlying structures and flow necessary to improve other recitations of mundane events in your life. Or don't memorize it. It was just a suggestion.

Technique #35

Choo! Choo! Get Onboard The Fun Express

When you're fortunate enough to be part of a playful chain of comments or entertaining group banter, make sure you know how to contribute and keep the fun train chugging along.

Real-life Examples

Joe described his new friend, Geoff, who planned to come over to the party later. Joe's friends added to his initial description.

> Joe: Yeah, be careful what you say, Geoff is a diehard vegan.
>
> Justin: Is he a big supporter of the anti-meat movements and stuff?
>
> Pat: I think he's actually part of an anti-meat movement.
>
> Randal: Actually, he *started the anti-meat movement!*

Why It Works

Wow, Geoff really got ganged up on there! This is an example of what I call an "escalation." Escalations are common with playful groups of people where everyone feeds off the humor of others. Sometimes, fun-loving comments occur in rapid-fire succession and it's hard to keep up.

Notice how it occurred: Joe started with a fairly strong label about Geoff. Justin added a supporting clarifying detail. Pat added a hypothetical. Randal seized on Pat's hypothetical and pushed it to the maximum limits of reality: Geoff isn't just part of the movement, he *started* the movement.

Escalations could also be referred to as the "Yes and..." activity—popular among improv comedians. It's a technique of continuing where someone else left off but taking it one step further. It's about asking the question: "If that's true, what else could be true?"

To escalate (or just continue) someone's comment requires a strong grasp of many of the humor techniques throughout this book. Hence, why this technique appears at the end—it's kind of like the final boss of humor. Don't feel bad if you can't always continue someone's playfulness—*it ain't easy being cheesy!* (Chester Cheetah reference anyone?)

Check out the following example. Each friend takes a turn adding a hypothetical statement that builds off the previous one.

> Maureen: Oh, you're only moving a few blocks down the street?
>
> Eileen: That's cool! That will make moving a lot easier.
>
> Kathleen: You could actually just put your furniture on a few dollies and roll it over there.
>
> Jolene: You're right! Or we could just get a mule.
>
> Maureen: I wonder where you could get a mule anyway— *Jed's Rent-a-Mule?*
>
> Eileen: I bet I could find one on Craigslist.
>
> Kathleen: Yeah, but I don't know if I'd want to buy anything from a guy selling mules online.

Could you keep the fun train going? Imagine the events actually occurring. Maybe speculate as to what would happen if you bought a mule from a guy online. "You might end up with _____" or "You may get to his house and find out he's _____."

Consider another example. A group of friends is at a petting zoo. They've been petting pigs, sheep, goats, cows—the whole Old MacDonald crew. Chad comes across a llama that just sits there motionless with its eyes closed. A simple sarcastic observation can be all it takes to plant the seed of humor. Notice how others play along:

> Chad: Wow, *llamas are so useful.*
>
> Lindsey: Yeah, his value is so underappreciated. People underestimate the number of uses for a llama.
>
> Ashley: Yeah! I heard they are really good at math. He's probably sitting there figuring out advanced algebra in his head.
>
> Lindsey: He's one of the last creatures that still understands how to use an abacus.
>
> Chad: How exactly would he use an abacus?
>
> Lindsey: With his tongue, of course.
>
> Chad: Of course. That makes perfect sense.

Lindsey and Ashley remained open to fun possibilities—if llamas are useful, what else could be true about them?

I was listening to the radio the other day and heard a great example of funny group banter. Apparently, a local high school student recently hacked the school and sent pornographic emails to all the parents. The exchange went as follows:

> Jon: That's incredible. When I was a student, I was lucky if I could get Microsoft Excel to add up some numbers for me!
>
> Ty: You know the FBI is going to show up and be like, 'Son, you're coming to work for us now.'

> Danny: Could you imagine what the Cyber Crime division looks like? It's probably just a bunch of 16-year-olds in a huge room.

> Arya: And the best part is they only need to get paid with pizza and Mountain Dew!

Notice that Danny had to first assume what Ty said was true. If it was true, what else could be true? Arya continued the trend. And then she sailed west of Westeros. (That reference was for you Game of Thrones fans!)

Play along with Yourself

I want to take a moment to revisit a few examples from the book because I'm not sure if you noticed something important. You may remember the following example from Technique #20:

I was working at my cubicle one day when a coworker, Patrick, came over and asked a question about my strange shark-fin looking computer mouse.

> Patrick: What kind of mouse is that?

> Me: It's ergonomic; it prevents you from getting carpal tunnel when you're older. You should try it.

What's the expected response here? That my friend would say something like, "Oh, that's cool. I could use one of those." Or, "That's nice, but I don't have any wrist issues." However, instead of the expected comments, my friend offered a perfect anti-premise that made me laugh:

> Patrick: Cool, but what if I *want* carpal tunnel when I'm older? I mean, it's always been a goal of mine to develop sore wrists.

Patrick could have stopped at the first line, but instead, added another supporting comment (his goal in life is to develop sore wrists). Remember, your initial funny remark will often benefit from a little support. If you anticipate a good reaction, feel free to embellish a little more and expand on the initial statement.

Let's review an example from Technique #21.

> Caitlyn: What was it that attracted you to me when we first met?
>
> Liam: I loved your infectious smile and your willingness to help everyone around you.

Was that funny? No, of course not. Caitlyn expected a serious/significant response, and Liam delivered. If Liam wanted to play with the premise, he could have gone to the extreme other end of the premise with something playful like the following:

> Liam: Honestly, I loved that you had five fingers on each hand. That was a huge turn on!
>
> Caitlyn: Oh, you shouldn't flatter me so much!
>
> Liam: I was getting sick of all those four-fingered women I kept dating. You showed up in my life and I was thrilled!

Notice that Liam kept the fun train going after his initial funny response about loving that she had five fingers. Assuming he was turned on by the fact that she had five fingers, what else could be true? *That he was getting sick and tired of dating all those four-fingered-women!* Liam could have mentioned how he fell for her tiny feet, the fact that she loved Cheetos, or some other trivial attraction.

Continue the Story

What about those situations where someone shares a personal or news story? Some stories are made even better when the listeners are active participants and help the storyteller along with additional comments and questions. In the following example, Michelle is just finishing up her quick story:

> Michelle: ...and I just wanted a small cup of water, but they made me pay for the normal-size fountain drink!
>
> Kenny: Really? What's the deal with that?

Kenny's response was good, but not funny good. How could Kenny exaggerate the event? I think Kenny deserves another shot.

> Kenny: Really? What's the deal with that? Like they can't afford to give you a cup just for water? *It's not like you're going to jump over the counter and steal some Sprite while they're not looking!*

Think about those times when someone just finishes telling a story or describing a particular situation, and you can't think of how to respond. Try inserting yourself into the situation or story. If you experienced the events in the story, how would you respond? How would you act? How would you be affected? Doing this will help you think of good hypothetical comments. Examine how Catherine puts herself into Mark's situation:

> Mark: And then the water started flooding my basement and I started seeing sparks—it was not good!
>
> Catherine: That scares the hell out of me. If I saw sparks and water, I'd be like 'Honey, *we need to get out of here! NOW!*'

A radio station I listen to features a morning show with three funny hosts. Since I'm slightly obsessed with studying humor techniques, I couldn't help but notice a few strategies they regularly employ in order to fill up airtime with humor. Every day, one of the hosts introduces a crazy story in the news, and the others take turns reacting to the story. For example:

> Host 1: Did you hear about that crazy girl who slashed her boyfriend's face because he wouldn't have sex with her?
>
> Host 2: What? That's *insane!*
>
> Host 1: Yeah, apparently, she sat on his neck so he couldn't resist. He eventually escaped and rushed to the hospital...
>
> Host 3: Well, I mean, she had to teach him a lesson if he wasn't being nice to her. He probably left the toilet seat up. That's what he gets for being so rude.
>
> Host 2: Maybe he was really into it and just wanted a new scar on his face. I mean, do we really know what the guy's into?
>
> Host 1: I couldn't imagine someone on my neck slashing at me. I'd be like, 'What the hell are you doing right now? We were just watching Netflix together like ten minutes ago and now you're on my neck?' Like, what do you do in that situation?

There you have it: three different and somewhat comical responses to a news story (with the understanding that the news story itself wasn't too funny). Let's break down each response and why it worked and how you can do it, too.

A. The story leads the listener down an expected path of sympathizing with the victim, so when Host 3 sides with the crazy antagonist in the story, it's essentially a reversal of the premise. It's understood that the woman is crazy, violent, and guilty of a horrible crime, so pretending like she's innocent and her crime is justified because of some trivial reason is not expected and could result in humor.

B. Host 2 gives the victim a ridiculous ulterior motive—also unexpected and potentially funny.

C. Host 1 puts himself in the situation and describes his reaction and thought process. He also paints a hypothetical scenario about the two of them watching Netflix right before the attack, resulting in a fun contrast against her violent actions.

These three types of reactions work for crazy news stories, but also for spicing up many other types of stories.

Group Banter and Meta Comments

The challenge with participating in group banter is how fast it can move; it's hard to keep up with multiple contributors. Obviously, all the chapters you read about up until now will help you navigate group banter, but meta comments should be your first priority if you need to buy time.

Sometimes groups will playfully pick on certain people and being armed with a riposte is ideal. However, clever comebacks are not always possible. Banter is sometimes a test to see if you know how to play along or if you become defensive instead. Protectively stating, "I'm offended by that. Please don't talk to me like that again," is code for, "Don't play around with me, I can't take a joke." Obviously, if you're truly being abused, you should speak up, but many people confuse frivolous banter with malicious teasing. Always try to play along when possible and appropriate.

That's where meta comments come in handy. Stepping back, and talking about what is being talked about, is easier and safer to do because you don't necessarily have to specifically address their message. Meta comments are perfect for whimsically letting someone know that you know how to play along, but that you also acknowledge that the other person is potentially crossing a line. Allow meta comments to help you deflect rather than get defensive and spoil any potential jolly mood.

> I was not ready for that much abuse this early in the morning.

> Is today pick-on-Jake-day or something?

> Oh no! I don't want any part of that.

> You always have to bring me into this, don't you?

> How did I know that was going to come back and haunt me?

Remember, if you don't allow people to joke with you once in a while, then they may not feel like joking when you're in the mood to be playful either. And worse, they may still joke about you, but it will be behind your back.

Homework

Funny often lives in the spontaneous. Try this exercise: Start with a topic, like *cats*, and see how long you can talk about anything related to cats without stopping. Keep adding "and..." to the end of your comments. It doesn't matter what topics or experiences or thoughts you connect to, just keep going. The point is to get you to open up your mind completely and become free of filters and worries. Here are some more random topics you should try once you're done with cats:

Ice cream

Halloween

Shoes

Volcano

Fence

School

Did you like that last exercise? See it performed by others on Nicholas Parsons' old BBC show "Just A Minute" where contestants had to talk for a minute about a random topic without hesitation, repetition, or deviation; it's quite entertaining. As of this writing, clips are still available on YouTube.

Want one more exercise to rev up your imagination? Think of a completely made-up word right now—a word that doesn't currently exist in any language. Got it? Good, now *define it.* What does it mean? Once you have a definition, *use it in a sentence.* Don't worry about how silly it sounds! Try again a few more times.

Final Homework: Study, Study, Study

L'esprit d'escalier ("staircase wit") is a French term for the predicament of coming up with a funny response two minutes too late. (Feel free to Google what "staircase" has to do with funny responses.) Has this ever happened to you? If it has, then you're in luck. If your mind is already generating funny responses, then you're close to responding in the moment rather than after the moment passes. The only thing lacking is practice. Like a sport, the more you practice, the faster your reaction time will become. Practice techniques with people you know or with complete strangers. Fine-tune *your* sense of humor.

Keep studying people who make *you* laugh. Learn their habits, their mannerisms, their lines, and study their timing and delivery. Get your hands on anything and everything you find funny and consume it like your mom told you not to. Biologists become biologists by reading and practicing biology, sports writers become sports writers by reading and writing about sports, and you're going to become a funnier person by reading, watching, listening to, and practicing humor.

Good comedians know how to take the mundane and make it funny. Situations you've encountered a hundred times, and don't see the funny in—they see it. Study comedians and enhance your ability to recognize the funny in everyday situations.

Play more. Play around with words and meanings. Just like how we discussed the importance of playing with the premise, wordplay (e.g., puns, innuendos, double-entendrés) relies on playing with underlying meanings. Wordplay didn't fit comfortably anywhere in this book, but because it's my Aunt

Sheila's favorite type of humor, I'd feel remiss if I didn't at least include a few examples. These are for you Aunt Sheila: "Don't trust atoms, they make up everything." And, "I'd tell you a chemistry joke, but I know I wouldn't get a good reaction."

As I was writing this section, one of my friends, Ben, texted me and asked if I wanted to participate in his March Madness bracket for $5. I replied, "I'm not a big bracket guy. Thanks, though." What was his response? He immediately replied, "What if I printed it really little?" He's a funny guy, so it didn't surprise me that he pounced on my word choice of "big" in order to make a funny wordplay. Ben's the kind of guy who's always looking for opportunities to be funny. Funny doesn't usually fall out trees and hit you on the head—it's an active process of looking and practicing.

You're not going to make everyone laugh, but you'll get along great with the people who do share your sense of humor. If you ever feel depressed about your comedic skills, check out the comments for comedians you like below their YouTube videos. Even the greatest comedians get torn apart by critics—no one is immune from criticism. There's no perfect comedian or perfect humor technique.

I was watching a very established, terrific comedian the other day on YouTube and most of the comments were along the lines of "He's hilarious." But then there were the "He sucks. He has more humor in his giant forehead," comments that quickly remind you of how complicated and difficult humor can be sometimes. Bottom line: you won't win over every crowd or every person, or even every cat for that matter. Actually, almost no cats will like you because cats don't like much of anything, so don't worry about cats.

In short, get yourself to the interwebs. Your first stop should be YouTube, and I want to emphasize the importance of watching and listening to the same thing *more than once*—it is the subsequent times watching and listening that you'll pick up on the nuances and techniques behind what the funny person is doing. If you can, memorize a few comedian's routines—you'll subconsciously pick up on subtle techniques without realizing it.

If I wasn't clear enough earlier, tell more stories. Start with super quick stories about recent everyday stuff—you'll become more comfortable with this in time. Your best stories will travel with you through life and, like fine wine, get better with age.

I'll leave you with a final real-life conversation to study on your own. I was recently at a Panera (one of my favorite work spots) and there was so much laughter coming from a table of four teenagers that I had to type out a portion of their group banter. It was almost like the Humor Gods placed them near me as I was wrapping up this book. Look for the exaggerations, labels, reactions, hypotheticals, quick stories, and meta comments. Maybe you'll even spot a new humor technique! I intentionally left out the names so you could focus on analyzing the comments. Enjoy!

That's a huge bite... are you starving or something?

I haven't eaten in like two hours. I'm totally starving. Don't sit too close to me or I might bite.

You seriously eat enough for three people. Three large, football playing type people.

Yummy... mine tastes like a soufflé.

I don't even know what a soufflé is... I'm not very cultured.

My ass is starting to hurt though.

Why do you have to say that? Don't pull the ass card on me.

This is normal for him.

Every time I hang out with you, I feel like I need to go home and take a shower.

I'm fairly sure I'm going to be sick an hour from now.

This isn't going to end well.

And I'll be laughing the entire time.

Hey, I didn't come here today just to have to take crap from you.

You guys have so much in common.

They say that love and hate are very close emotions. It's something they say.

Who's they?

You know... people who know things... *psychologists.*

You guys mind if I take a Snapchat?

Go for it. But only my good side.

I'm gonna zoom right in on your nose. You're going to hate me for this!

If you post that I'm going to neck-punch you... like twice.

It had better be good.

I saw Lizzy yesterday at the Panera on 5th street, it was really weird... I was like, 'What are you doing here? *You're not supposed to be here.* I thought you were in college.'

That would have been awkward... I didn't think you two were talking anymore...

I could tell she was judging my sandwich too. I was like, 'Screw you, Lizzy... I don't need your opinion... no one asked...' And I decided to be polite, but I could have been much worse; sarcasm is my primary language.

That Panera is really busy anyway, I hate going to that one.

And all the weirdos go there.

I'd never go there again. Why are you hanging out with weirdos?

Let's get out of here... should we just leave everything here?

No, that's SOOO lazy.

Won't they pick it up?

Are you gonna bring your drink at least?

Yeah why not, I like walking around with drinks.

Can you carry mine too? You'd make a great bartender.

Except I don't like alcohol. I'd only serve soda and ice teas.

Your bar would last like two weeks before it shut down.

You're right, I need a new life goal.

Did you notice any techniques? I hope so! If I were your teacher I'd ask you to find ten techniques within that conversation. But I'm not your teacher, and you're going to do whatever the hell you want.

In all seriousness, the world needs *less* seriousness, and *more* laughter. If you make even one more person laugh because of this book, that would make my day.

P.S. Smile more.

P.P.S. But don't smile all the time. That's just creepy.

Recommended Viewing

From Technique #2

Jennifer Lawrence

She's likeable and funny because she's a master of self-deprecating humor. You won't find many Hollywood actors as genuine and quick to point out personal flaws as her.

> MsMojo. "Top 10 Funniest Jennifer Lawrence Moments,"
> YouTube Video, March 1, 2018,
> https://www.youtube.com/watch?v=s12nFqnzUc4.

From Technique #3

Aziz Ansari

Try focusing on his delivery. Study *how* he talks. Then mute the video and observe *how* he communicates with his body language. Notice how he's interesting to watch even when you can't hear him.

> Netflix, "Aziz Ansari: Live at Madison Square Garden –
> Plans with Flaky People – Netflix Is A Joke," YouTube
> Video, March 12, 2015,
> https://www.youtube.com/watch?v=_RbMv7HUiO4.

Tina Fey

Watch some YouTube clips of her talking about her daughters. She can tell a simple story about snot falling on a shoe and still keep the audience engaged. If you get a chance, watch the video again, but mute it and pay attention to her amazingly expressive body language.

> The Tonight Show Starring Jimmy Fallon, "Tina Fey's
> Impression of Her Daughter," YouTube Video, March 1,
> 2014, https://www.youtube.com/watch?v=iVh7KJW0cFU

From Technique #7

Candace Payne

In 2016, Candace Payne became famous for her reaction to a Chewbacca mask. That's seriously it. Reactions are powerful.

> Jon Deak, "Laughing Chewbacca Mask Lady," YouTube
> Video, May 19, 2016,
> https://www.youtube.com/watch?v=y3yRv5Jg5TI.

Shane Dawson

There's a lot of stuff here to digest and I'll be honest, some videos are too intense for me, but he's still worth learning from. There are a ton of reaction videos where he plays video games, tests out food, mocks weird toys, and much more.

> https://www.youtube.com/user/shane

From Technique #8

Check out YouTubers who review things. Start with *Shut Up & Sit Down* and see what YouTube rabbit hole that leads you down:

> https://www.youtube.com/channel/UCyRhIGDUKdIOw07
> Pd8pHxCw

From Technique #12

Aziz Ansari

A few simple details are sometimes all it takes to make the hypothetical come to life. Fast forward to around the one-minute mark in the following video. He doesn't just ask you to imagine sitting by yourself in a chair; he says imagine sitting by yourself in a wooden chair... eating a can of beans.

> Netflix, "Aziz Ansari: Live at Madison Square Garden –
> Plans with Flaky People – Netflix Is A Joke," YouTube
> Video, March 12, 2015,
> https://www.youtube.com/watch?v=_RbMv7HUiO4.

From Technique #18

President Obama

Watch President Obama perfectly execute The Rule of Three. Talking about salmon creates a pattern, which sets up the third, unexpected punchline.

> CNN, "CNN: SOTU Address, President Obama cracks
> smoked salmon joke," YouTube Video, January 25, 2011,
> https://www.youtube.com/watch?v=BFcWz9eyovA.

From Technique #20

A simple, classic example of playing with the premise (or subtext) and how humor requires awareness of what's understood below the surface.

> Rudolph Smith, "We'll Make Spears," YouTube Video scene
> from Braveheart (1995), December 8, 2016,
> https://www.youtube.com/watch?v=pqRqvmn1MqQ.

From Technique #22

Jerry Seinfeld

> Dothelper, "Seinfeld The Yada Yada: Anti-Dentite,"
> YouTube Video, October 13, 2006,
> https://www.youtube.com/watch?v=ythrdCsOFJU.

Watch *Comedians in Cars Getting Coffee* (Netflix, 2012 - present). A perfect show to learn about conversational humor. When you mix Jerry with other comedians in casual environments, you get comedy gold.

Mystery Science Theater 3000 (Netflix, 2017)

For a great demonstration of observational comedians in action, check out Mystery Science Theater 3000 on Netflix. If you're not familiar with the comedy series, its premise is simple: a few comedians watch old B movies and humorously comment on the film the entire time (also referred to as "riffing"). You can study first-hand how masters of observational comedy react to events in real-time. If you watch the show, try to come up with your own commentary as a good practice exercise!

From Technique #24

Conan O'Brien

A master of observations and hypotheticals, Conan knows how to keep conversations perpetually in the play zone. He's in his element with his friend Tim Olyphant. Check out the podcast and YouTube clips below.

> Timothy Olyphant, guest. "Conan O'Brien Needs a Friend."
> Podcast audio. Team Coco. February 17, 2019.

Team Coco, "Timothy Olyphant Copies Conan's New Look –
CONAN on TBS," YouTube Video, March 13, 2019,
https://www.youtube.com/watch?v=6-lg5-ou59g

Conan has a great series where he reviews games:

Team Coco, *"Clueless Gamer: Conan Reviews "Super Smash
Bros."* YouTube Video, July 11, 2014,
https://www.youtube.com/watch?v=_1hkSUGgPC8.

While reviewing Super Smash Bros, he adds a strong label to the
Villager character (@ 4:00min), "Look at his eyes, those are the eyes of
a killer." Painting the innocent Villager character as a killer sets up
the potential for follow-up funny hypothetical comments for the rest
of the conversation. His first follow-up hypothetical comment was,
"...he's enraged because a mad scientist put spoons on his hands."

From Technique #27

There's a scene in the comedy, *Talladega Nights: The Ballad of Ricky Bobby*
(Sony Pictures, 2006), in which Will Ferrell (Ricky Bobby) is being
interviewed and doesn't know what to do with his hands. He casually
admits, "I'm not sure what to do with my hands." Moments later, his
hands come floating back up into view again. That scene is arguably
one of the most referenced scenes of any comedy in history. Even
thirteen years later, I still hear it referenced in casual conversation on
a regular basis. Why? Not knowing what to do with our hands is a
situation we've probably all experienced at some point and can relate
to. (Will Ferrell exaggerated the situation perfectly.) Similarly, have
you ever felt anxious about the proper way to sit during a job
interview? Or ever wondered to yourself how much you should eat
during a first date? Or if a first kiss was appropriate? Calling attention

to the awkwardness of a social situation (with meta comments) releases the unspoken tension and often sparks humor and laughs.

> Alexish1175, "Talladega Nights Rickey Bobby Camera Interview... WHOOOO!" YouTube Video, March 16, 2009, https://www.youtube.com/watch?v=M8PP3QU7wjI.

From Technique #29

Check out any of the *Conan O'Brien Needs a Friend* podcasts. He's not only a comedic genius and improv master, but he's perfected the art of keeping conversations engaging and entertaining with personal and cultural references. Where many comedians need to write and plan jokes, Conan ad libs comedy gold on the fly.

From Technique #33

Robin Williams

A good breakdown of his comedic style:

> Charisma on Command, "Robin Williams' #1 Tip to Becoming Funnier," YouTube Video, March 10, 2016, https://www.youtube.com/watch?v=WNXvFG98npU&vl=e n-US.

Also check him out in the following video, between the 8:00 – 9:10 minute mark. He brilliantly imitates multiple people.

> The Graham Norton Show, "World's Funniest Comics on The Graham Norton Show | Volume 1," YouTube Video, August 4, 2018, https://www.youtube.com/watch?v=OEJcj-RMp3k.

Greg Davies

During the aforementioned video, a little later, between 10:00 – 12:00 minutes, Greg Davies' story about wearing his mother's underwear is probably one of the funniest stories ever told on The Graham Norton show. But if you watch it, you'll probably notice how unfunny the first half of his story was. He dared to spend the entire first minute just building up the story, which is long for someone on a televised show, and you can almost feel the other people thinking, "Get on with it, will ya, Greg??" But notice how he quickly recovered from a slow beginning by introducing multiple hilarious reactions to the turning point, including: *his own mental reaction, his physical reaction, and how others reacted.* He was able to transport the listeners to those moments he described so colorfully and enthusiastically. He turned an otherwise average story into a memorable masterpiece.

Jim Gaffigan

YouTube Jim and listen to how he slips into a few other voices so effortlessly. I recommend starting with:

> jimgaffigan, " Jim Gaffigan – Cake – Beyond the Pale,"
> YouTube Video, March 12, 2009,
> https://www.youtube.com/watch?v=-o-u4IwXkbE

Aziz Ansari

And you know by now I'm a huge fan of Aziz Ansari—you'll find his impersonations, characters, and inner monologue awesome too.

Bonus Viewing

Sir Ken Robinson

Ken has contributed a lot to society, but he's never been known as a comedian, so why would I include him here? Because he currently holds the record for the most popular TED talk of all time. And there's a reason for that. Besides the important message of his presentation, his delivery and humor are utterly captivating. I couldn't squeeze his speech into one technique category, because he effortlessly weaves so many techniques into his presentation. And unlike traditional comedy acts where a lot of the techniques don't transfer to real-life, Ken's humor is more conversational and applicable to everyday conversation. Treat his talk like a Comedic Easter Egg hunt and see how many humor techniques you can find! Study why the audience laughs when they do. Maybe you'll discover a new technique that I didn't mention yet?

> TED, "Do schools kill creativity? | Sir Ken Robinson,"
> YouTube Video, January 6, 2007,
> https://www.youtube.com/watch?v=iG9CE55wbtY.

Robin Williams

Here's another oldie but a goodie. The funniest moments are rarely ever planned or rehearsed, but instead, occur when a person versed in comedic techniques encounters an interesting situation. Check out what happens when the great Robin Williams misses out on the award but has a chance to speak nonetheless (about midway through the video). I gave up trying to count all the humor techniques!

> broadcastfilmcritics, "Daniel Day Lewis, Jack Nicholson
> (Robin Williams) Accepting Critics' Choice Award,"
> YouTube Video, July 20, 2009,
> https://www.youtube.com/watch?v=bb7303ukNtk.

Made in the USA
Middletown, DE
25 November 2019

79342346R00149